EXCEL PIVOT TABLES

Basic Beginners Guide
to Learn Excel Pivot Tables
for Data Analysis and Modeling

MG Martin

TABLE OF CONTENTS

Introduction

I want to thank you for choosing this book, 'Excel Pivot Tables - Basic Beginners Guide to Learn Excel Pivot Tables for Data Analysis and Modeling.'

Most organizations and businesses use Excel to perform data analysis. These organizations also use it for modeling. There are numerous features and add-ins that Excel offers which make it easier to perform data analysis and modeling. A pivot table is one such feature provided by Excel.

You can analyze a million rows of data within a few clicks, show the required results, create a pivot chart or report, drag the necessary fields around and highlight the necessary information. It is imperative that people who use excel are well versed with using pivots. If you are looking to learn more about what a pivot table is and how you can use it for data analysis, you have come to the right place.

Over the course of the book, you will learn more about what a pivot table is, how you can create a pivot table, the different ways you can use a pivot table and much more. The information in the book is easy to understand and will guide you on how you can use a pivot table to analyze data.

Thank you for purchasing the book. I hope you gather the information you are looking for.

Chapter 1

An Introduction to Pivot Tables

A pivot table is one of the most powerful tools or features that Excel offers. You can extract a significant amount of information from a large data set using a pivot table. For the purpose of this chapter, we will be using a data set that contains 213 rows and 6 headers or fields namely, Order ID, Product, Category, Amount, Date and Country.

	A	B	C	D	E	F	G	H
1	Order ID	Product	Category	Amount	Date	Country		
2	1	Carrots	Vegetables	$4,270	1/6/2016	United States		
3	2	Broccoli	Vegetables	$8,239	1/7/2016	United Kingdom		
4	3	Banana	Fruit	$617	1/8/2016	United States		
5	4	Banana	Fruit	$8,384	1/10/2016	Canada		
6	5	Beans	Vegetables	$2,626	1/10/2016	Germany		
7	6	Orange	Fruit	$3,610	1/11/2016	United States		
8	7	Broccoli	Vegetables	$9,062	1/11/2016	Australia		
9	8	Banana	Fruit	$6,906	1/16/2016	New Zealand		
10	9	Apple	Fruit	$2,417	1/16/2016	France		
11	10	Apple	Fruit	$7,421	1/16/2016	Canada		

Let us now look at how we can insert a pivot table to organize the data set.

Insert a Pivot Table

You should follow the steps mentioned below if you want to insert a pivot table in Excel.

1. Select any cell that is within the data set.

2. Go to the tab 'Insert' and check the 'Tables' group. Click the 'Pivot Table' option.

3. You will see the dialog box below on your screen. If you look clearly at the image below, you will notice that Excel has automatically selected the data for you. Excel always chooses the default location for a pivot as a New Worksheet.

4. Click OK.

You will see that a New Worksheet has opened with a pivot table that is linked to your data set. Alternatively, you can instruct Excel to create the pivot table in the same worksheet if needed.

Drag Fields in a Pivot

Once you create the pivot table, you will see the Pivot Table pane appear on the right side of your screen. For the purpose of this example, we want to calculate the total amount that was exported for each product. To do this, you will need to drag the following fields into the different areas at the bottom of the Pivot Table pane.

1. Amount field in Values Area.

2. Product field in Rows Area.

3. Country field in the Filters Area.

Your Pivot Table panel will now look like the image below:

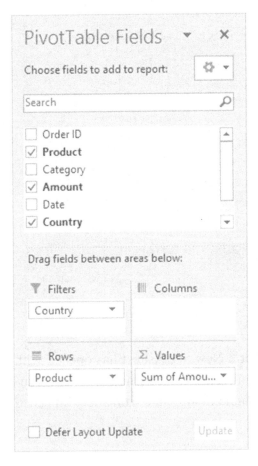

You will see that the pivot table has been created in the Excel sheet. This is how easy it is to create and use a pivot table. From the pivot table that was created, you will notice that the main export is Bananas.

	A	B	C
1	Country	(All)	
2			
3	Row Labels	Sum of Amount	
4	Apple	191257	
5	Banana	340295	
6	Beans	57281	
7	Broccoli	142439	
8	Carrots	136945	
9	Mango	57079	
10	Orange	104438	
11	Grand Total	1029734	
12			

Sort Data in a Pivot

Once you create the pivot, you may want to sort the data to ensure that you have sorted the data, in the example above, let us look at how we can move Bananas to the top of the table.

1. Go to any cell under the column labeled Sum of Amount.

2. Right click on the column and click on the Sort option. Now, select the 'Sort Largest to Smallest' option.

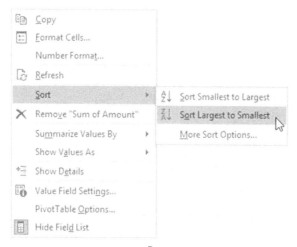

3. You will obtain the following result.

	A	B	C
1	Country	(All)	
2			
3	Row Labels	Sum of Amount	
4	Banana	340295	
5	Apple	191257	
6	Broccoli	142439	
7	Carrots	136945	
8	Orange	104438	
9	Beans	57281	
10	Mango	57079	
11	Grand Total	1029734	
12			

Filter the Pivot

Now that we have included the Field Country as a filter, you can now filter the pivot based on the country that is available in the data set. For instance, you can check the different products that are mostly exported in France.

1. Go to the drop down arrow in the filter section of the pivot and choose the option 'France.'

2. You will see that apples are the main products exported from France.

	A	B	C
1	Country	France	
2			
3	Row Labels	Sum of Amount	
4	Apple	80193	
5	Banana	36094	
6	Carrots	9104	
7	Mango	7388	
8	Broccoli	5341	
9	Orange	2256	
10	Beans	680	
11	Grand Total	141056	
12			

Alternatively, you can also use the triangle arrow that is present next to Row Labels to filter on the products. This will, however, only show you the amounts of the different products that are exported.

Change Summary Calculation

Excel uses a default option when it is summarizing your data. It will either count the items or sum them up. If you want to change the calculation that is being performed, you should follow the steps given below:

1. Go to any cell within the column 'Sum of Amount.'

2. Right click on the column and choose the option 'Value Field Settings.'

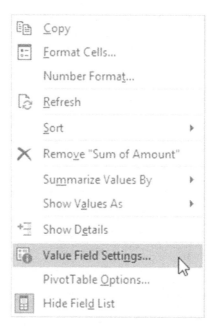

3. Now, choose the calculation that you want to use. You have multiple options to choose from. Let us choose the 'Count' option for the purpose of this example.

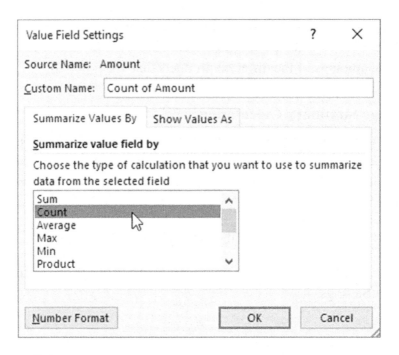

4. Click OK.

	A	B	C
1	Country	France 〽	
2			
3	Row Labels ⤓	Count of Amount	
4	Apple	16	
5	Banana	7	
6	Carrots	1	
7	Mango	1	
8	Orange	1	
9	Beans	1	
10	Broccoli	1	
11	Grand Total	28	
12			

Alternatively, you can change the calculation using the fields present in the Pivot Table pane.

Two-Dimensional Pivot Table

You can create a two-dimensional pivot table by dragging a field to both the Rows and Columns area in the pivot table pane. Before you do this, you will need to create a pivot table. Let us now calculate the amount of product exported to different countries using a two-dimensional pivot table. Follow the steps below to do this

1. Move the country field to the row area.

2. Move the product field to the columns area.

3. Move to Amount field to the values area.

4. Move the category field to the filters area.

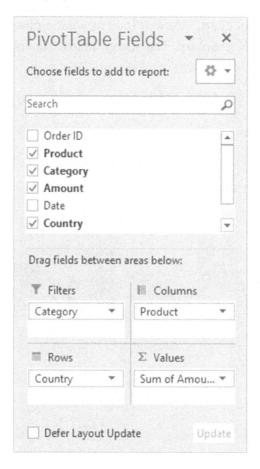

The following image depicts a two-dimensional pivot table.

	A	B	C	D	E	F	G	H	I	J
1	Category	(All)								
2										
3	Sum of Amount	Column								
4	Row Labels	Apple	Banana	Beans	Broccoli	Carrots	Mango	Orange	Grand Total	
5	Australia	20634	52721	14433	17953	8106	9186	8680	131713	
6	Canada	24867	33775		12407		3767	19929	94745	
7	France	80193	36094	680	5341	9104	7388	2256	141056	
8	Germany	9082	39686	29905	37197	21636	8775	8887	155168	
9	New Zealand	10332	40050		4390			12010	66782	
10	United Kingdom	17534	42908	5100	38436	41815	5600	21744	173137	
11	United States	28615	95061	7163	26715	56284	22363	30932	267133	
12	Grand Total	191257	340295	57281	142439	136945	57079	104438	1029734	
13										

When you want to compare numbers, you can apply the same filters and create a pivot chart. We will look at what a pivot chart is in detail in the subsequent chapters. The image below shows you how a pivot chart looks.

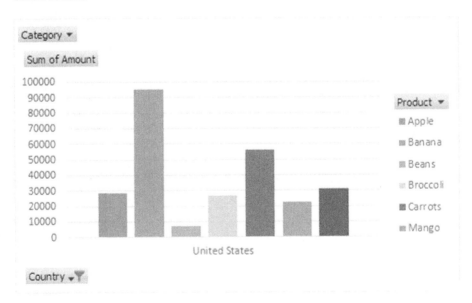

Chapter 2

Advantages and Disadvantages
of Pivot Tables

A ccording to https://connectusfund.org/8-advantages-and-dis-advantages-of-pivot-tables, "Pivot tables are program tools that allow users to summarize or reorganize rows or columns of data. They are usually found in database tables and spreadsheets, allowing for information to be obtained from the report without the need for the file to be altered."

Here are some of the advantages and disadvantages of using a tool like a pivot table in your tables.

Advantages of Pivot Tables

Allow Users To View How Data Works

A pivot table is one of the many Excel tools that allow a user to obtain some deep insights into data. You can generate multiple reports in Excel using this tool using one data set.

Works Well With SQL Exports

If you insert a pivot table in Microsoft Excel, you can work with that pivot table on any SQL export.

Data Is Easier To Segment

It is easier to gather some analytics about the data set into a database or spreadsheet using a pivot table.

You Can Generate Instant Data

You can create instant data using a pivot table regardless of whether you use an equation to obtain that information or you rely only on formulae.

Disadvantages of Pivot Tables

A Time-Consuming Venture

For most forms of data analyses, it is a good idea to use pivot tables since you are able to obtain the data that you want to understand. You can obtain the required metrics to understand the data. That being said, a pivot table does not include all the necessary calculation options. This means that you will need to use equations or manual calculations to obtain the required information, and you will need to input the required data manually. This will take up a sufficient amount of time.

No Automatic Updates

Pivot tables do not automatically update when there is a change to the data set. So, when you run a report on a pivot table, you will need to refresh the pivot table to obtain the right analytics or metrics. A program that uses pivot tables does not always allow you to summarize the information easily.

Difficult For Older Computers To Present The Data

If the database you are using or the spreadsheet you are using is large, it can be difficult for old computers to produce the right analytics. It is possible that the system crashes because of the sheer volume of data. This is because the processing power of the system cannot handle the requirements.

It Is Difficult To Learn

It is easy for people to learn how to create and use a pivot table, but it is hard to understand how you can present that information in a way that it can be used. A spreadsheet often does not focus on the presentation of data in a pivot table.

A pivot table is a good option to use for small data sets, but it is hard to use for a large data set. When you take these pros and cons into account, you will know how to organize the data well in a spreadsheet and use it.

Chapter 3

What Can You Do With Pivot Tables?

There are numerous actions that one can perform using pivot tables. This chapter throws some light on the different functions you can perform using Pivot tables. Please download the workbook we will be using for the examples in this chapter from the following link: https://www.myexcelonline.com/wp-content/uploads/2017/02/Sort-by-Largest-or-Smallest.xlsx

Working with Tables

A table is another powerful Excel feature, and it has many advantages. Regardless of the size of your data, it is important that you use them since the benefits of using tables are countless.

1. Tables allow structured referencing.

2. You can build tables with existing conditional formats.

3. You can calculate the totals of a column by using the Total row option. This option will use a formula to calculate the total.

4. You can sort and filter the data using drop down lists.

5. The column letters or content are replaced by the header when you are scrolling down a column.

6. You can remove any duplicate row from the table easily.

7. Summarize the information in the table using a pivot table.

8. You can create columns using dynamic formulae in the pivot table.

Step One: Select any cell in the table.

CUSTOMER	REGION	ORDER DATE	SALES	MONTH	YEAR
Acme, inc.	NORTH	2014-04-13	$55,815	April	2014
Widget Corp	SOUTH	2014-12-21	$94,908	December	2014
123 Warehousing	EAST	2014-02-15	$57,088	February	2014
Demo Company	WEST	2014-05-14	$56,539	May	2014
Smith and Co.	NORTH	2015-06-28	$63,116	June	2015
Foo Bars	SOUTH	2015-01-15	$38,281	January	2015
ABC Telecom	EAST	2015-08-22	$57,650	August	2015
Fake Brothers	WEST	2015-12-31	$90,967	December	2015

Step Two: Now, insert a table for the data that you have in your sheet. To do this, go to Tab 'Insert' and select the option 'Table'

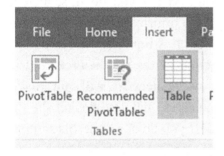

Step Three: Ensure that you select the dialog box that says 'My table has headers.' Click Ok.

15

You now have a table ready.

CUSTOMER	REGION	ORDER DATE	SALES	MONTH	YEAR
Acme, inc.	NORTH	2014-04-13	$55,815	April	2014
Widget Corp	SOUTH	2014-12-21	$94,908	December	2014
123 Warehousing	EAST	2014-02-15	$57,088	February	2014
Demo Company	WEST	2014-05-14	$56,539	May	2014
Smith and Co.	NORTH	2015-06-28	$63,116	June	2015
Foo Bars	SOUTH	2015-01-15	$38,281	January	2015
ABC Telecom	EAST	2015-08-22	$57,650	August	2015
Fake Brothers	WEST	2015-12-31	$90,967	December	2015

Focus on Auditing the Data

When you want to perform data analysis in Excel, regardless of the method you choose to analyze the data, you must look at the different attributes that make up a specific value. To do this, you should double-click on the cell that contains the value. When you do this, a new worksheet is created which will contain the information of all the rows or data that are used to calculate that value. It is important to remember that this information is a simple extraction of the data source, and if you edit the information in the new worksheet, it will not make changes to the pivot table. All the changes that you make should always be made to the main data source. If you do not want this sample data, you can either press delete or undo. You can double-click on any value that is present in the Pivot table, including the subtotals and totals.

Step One: Select a cell in the pivot table, and double click on that cell.

Row Labels	Sum of SALES
EAST	2,057,650
NORTH	1,063,116
SOUTH	1,538,281
WEST	2,590,967
Grand Total	**7,250,014**

Sum of SALES
Value: 2,590,967
Row: WEST

▶ ▶| Sheet1 | **Pivot Table** |

You will see that a new worksheet has opened which provides information about the selected cell. As mentioned earlier, any change made in this new worksheet will not change the original data source or the data in the pivot.

	A	B	C	D	E	F
1	CUSTOMER ▼	REGION ▼	ORDER DATE ▼	SALES ▼	MONTH ▼	YEAR ▼
2	Fake Brothers	WEST	31/12/2015	90967	December	2015
3	Demo Compan	WEST	14/05/2014	2500000	May	2014
4						

Refreshing the Pivot

It is important to remember to refresh the data in your pivot table whenever you make a change to the source data. Whenever you update any information in the data source, you must refresh the pivot table to ensure that the changes are flowing through. You can do this in three different ways:

- Go to the PivotTable tools section, go to the options section and click refresh.

- Use the shortcut Alt+F5.

- Right click on any cell in the pivot table and choose the option to refresh the table in the dialog box that opens.

Step One: Make a change to a value in the data set.

CUSTOMER	REGION	ORDER DATE	SALES	MONTH	YEAR
Acme, inc.	NORTH	13/04/2014	$1,000,000	April	2014
Widget Corp	SOUTH	21/12/2014	$1,500,600	December	2014
123 Warehousing	EAST	15/02/2014	$2,000,000	February	2014
Demo Company	WEST	14/05/2014	2500000	May	2014
Smith and Co.	NORTH	28/06/2015	$63,116	June	2015
Foo Bars	SOUTH	15/01/2015	$38,281	January	2015
ABC Telecom	EAST	22/08/2015	$57,650	August	2015
Fake Brothers	WEST	31/12/2015	$90,967	December	2015

Step Two: Now, click the pivot table.

Sum of SALES	Column Labels ▾		
Row Labels ▾	2014	2015	Grand Total
EAST	29923	57650	87573
NORTH	24640	63116	87756
SOUTH	24640	38281	62921
WEST	66901	90967	157868
Grand Total	146104	250014	396118

Step Three: Right click on any cell in the pivot table, and hit the refresh button.

Sum of SALES	Column Labels ▾		
Row Labels ▾	2014	2015	
EAST	29923	57650	
NORTH	24640	63116	
SOUTH	24640	38281	
WEST	66901	90967	
Grand Total	146104	25001	

Calibri ▾ 11 ▾ A A 🖩 ▾ % , 🔢
B I ≡ 🖉 ▾ A ▾ ⊞ ▾ .0 .00 ✧

- 📋 Copy
- 📑 Format Cells...
-    Number Format...
- 📄 Refresh ⌖
-    Sort ▸
- ✕ Remove 'Sum of SALES'

You will see that the values in the pivot table have been updated.

Sum of SALES	Column Labels ▾		
Row Labels ▾	2014	2015	Grand Total
EAST	2000000	57650	2057650
NORTH	1000000	63116	1063116
SOUTH	1500000	38281	1538281
WEST	2500000	90967	2590967
Grand Total	7000000	250014	7250014

Subtotals

If you have multiple fields in the Rows area in the pivot table, you will notice that there is a Subtotal option under every group in the pivot. So, what if you want to remove the option to view the subtotals at the bottom of the group or want to show the values at the top of the group? You can work with subtotals in different ways. Let us look at how you can do this.

Step One: Move at least two fields in the Row labels area in the pivot table pane.

Step Two: Now, click on your pivot table, and move to the PivotTable Tools option. Choose the Design option and move to the subtotals section.

Step Three: Now, choose one of the following options:

Do Not Show Subtotals	

Row Labels	Sum of SALES
2014	
EAST	2,000,000
NORTH	1,000,000
SOUTH	1,500,000
WEST	2,500,000
2015	
EAST	57,650
NORTH	63,116
SOUTH	38,281
WEST	90,967
Grand Total	7,250,014

Row Labels	Sum of SALES
2014	
EAST	2,000,000
NORTH	1,000,000
SOUTH	1,500,000
WEST	2,500,000
2014 Total	**7,000,000**
2015	
EAST	57,650
NORTH	63,116
SOUTH	38,281
WEST	90,967
2015 Total	**250,014**
Grand Total	**7,250,014**

Show all Subtotals at Top of Group

Row Labels	Sum of SALES
2014	**7,000,000**
EAST	2,000,000
NORTH	1,000,000
SOUTH	1,500,000
WEST	2,500,000
2015	**250,014**
EAST	57,650
NORTH	63,116
SOUTH	38,281
WEST	90,967
Grand Total	**7,250,014**

20

Report Layouts

Your report can be in three different layouts – outline, tabular and compact. Choose a layout by going to the option PivotTable Tools. Choose Design and click on Report Layouts. Each of these layouts has its own pros and cons, and we will look at each of them below in detail.

Compact Layout

You can use this layout to optimize the data for readability since it allows you to keep the data related to the pivot in one column. It will be hard to do the analysis in the future if you copy the data into a new worksheet.

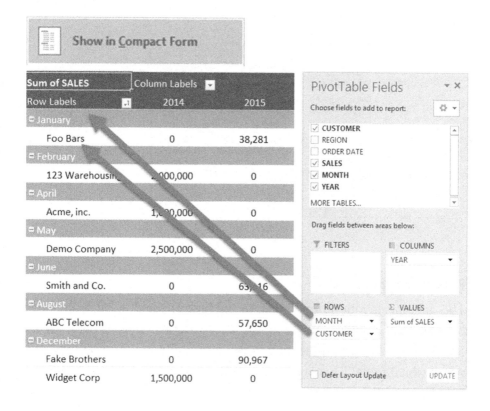

Outline Layout

This layout will allow you to include a field's header in every column. You can also repeat every label in the data set when you use this layout. Unlike the compact layout, the outline layout allows you to reuse the source data in any new location for other types of analysis. The disadvantage is that this layout occupies too much space.

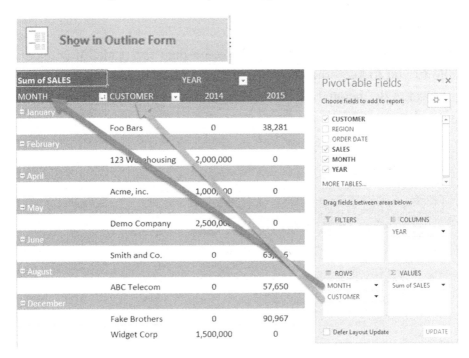

Tabular Layout

The tabular layout allows you to include a field header in every column, and allows you to repeat every item that is present in the labels. You will see all the data in the source file in the same format as a traditional table. This layout, much like the outline layout occupies a lot of space. It is also very difficult to include a subtotal at the top of the group.

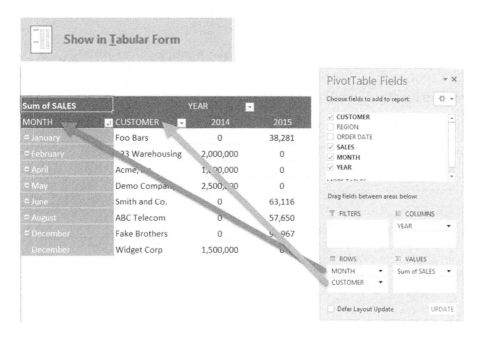

Change the Value Field Setting

Most users complain that they only get the count of the values instead the sum of those values. There are three reasons why this happens:

- Your source data includes blank cells.

- The columns with values in them show that there are text fields within the column.

- There are grouped data in the source data.

Blank Cells

There may be an issue where you have blank cells or missing data in the source data. When there are blanks in the source data, Excel will automatically assume that the entire column is text based.

SALES REGION	ORDER DATE	SALES	FINANCIAL YEAR
AMERICAS	13/04/2012	24,640	2012
AMERICAS	21/12/2012	24,640	2012
AMERICAS	24/12/2012	29,923	2012
AMERICAS	24/12/2012	66,901	2012
AMERICAS	29/12/2012		2012
AMERICAS	28/06/2012	38,281	2012
AMERICAS	28/06/2012	57,650	2012
AMERICAS	29/06/2012	90,967	2012
AMERICAS	29/06/2012	11,910	2012
AMERICAS	06/07/2012	59,531	2012
AMERICAS	06/07/2012	88,297	2012

Text Cells

If there are some cells that have been formatted as text in the values column in the pivot pane, Excel will not calculate the sum of the values in those cells, but will count them instead. This happens when you download the information from an external system or the Internet. This is because these sources often convert numbers into text.

SALES REGION	ORDER DATE	SALES	FINANCIAL YEAR
AMERICAS	13/04/2012	24,640	2012
AMERICAS	21/12/2012	24,640	2012
AMERICAS	24/12/2012	29,923	2012
AMERICAS	24/12/2012	66,901	2012
AMERICAS	29/12/2012	2,556	2012
AMERICAS	28/06/2012	38281P	2012
AMERICAS	28/06/2012	57,650	2012
AMERICAS	29/06/2012	90,967	2012
AMERICAS	29/06/2012	11,910	2012

In such situations, you will get only the count of the sales and not the total sales amount.

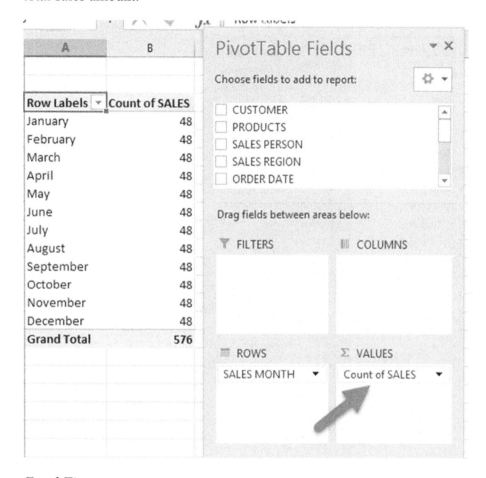

Excel Fix

Step One: Enter either a zero or any other value in the blank cell or the cells formatted as text.

Step Two: Click on the column that is formatted as text in the pivot, and right click on any cell in that column. Remove this column from the Values area in the pivot pane.

Step Three: Refresh the pivot table.

Step Four: Add the column to the values field in the area once again.

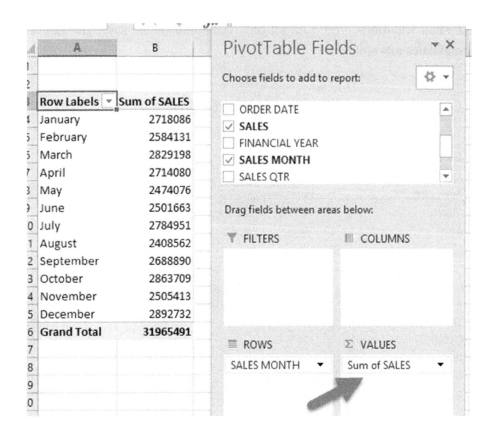

Grouped Values

Let us assume that you have included sales or a similar number in the Values field in the row and column areas of the pivot pane, and you want to group it. When you drop those values in the field, you will get the option to count the number of variables.

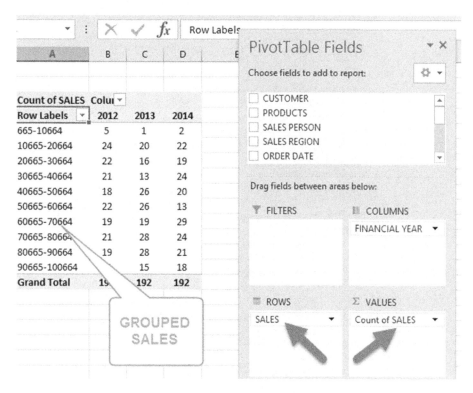

Excel Fix:

Step One: You should first ungroup the values in the pivot table. To do this, right click on the grouped values and choose the 'ungroup' option.

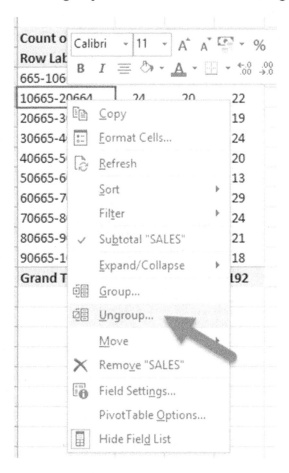

Step Two: Now, drag the count of the sales from the Value area and move it back to the original section of the pivot table pane.

Step Thee: Move the Sales field back into the Values area of the pivot table pane.

This will not show you a sum of all the sales.

Sum of SALES	Column Labels				PivotTable Fields
Row Labels	2012	2013	2014		
665	665				Choose fields to add to report:
2,545	2,545				
2,556	2,556				☐ SALES PERSON
10,014		10,014			☐ SALES REGION
10,090	10,090				☐ ORDER DATE
10,209			10,209		☑ SALES
10,282			10,282		☐ TRANSACTIONS
10,338	10,338				
10,690		10,690			Drag fields between areas below:
10,780	10,780				
10,907		10,907			▼ FILTERS ▦ COLUMNS
11,014		11,014			FINANCIAL YEAR ▼
11,136	11,136				
11,145	11,145				
11,317			11,317		
11,347	11,347				▤ ROWS Σ VALUES
11,497			11,497		SALES ▼ Sum of SALES ▼
11,910	11,910				
12,024		12,024			
12,429	12,429				

It is important to remember that you will sometimes need to verify if the pivot table includes any values that are grouped. It may not be evident to the naked eye, especially if the data is not selected in either the row or column labels.

If you want to confirm that the fields have been grouped, you should move this field from the Pivot Table field into the row or column label area.

Number Formatting

It is easy to format the values in the pivot table by choosing the number format option. You can change the format of the number to a number, percentage, currency and custom.

Step One: Right click on a cell in the pivot table that contains a number, and choose the option 'Number format.'

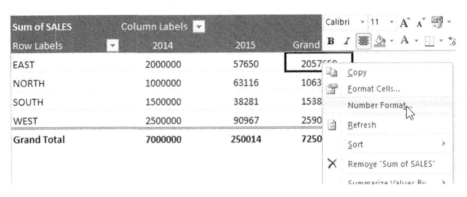

Step Two: You should now choose the format that you want to use.

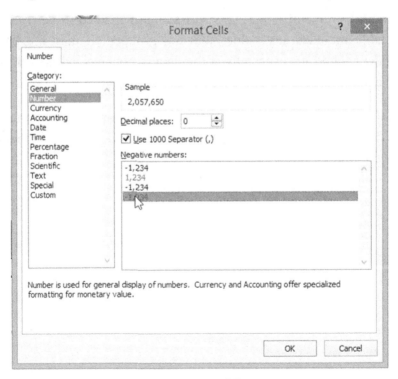

The number formatting in your pivot table has been updated based on the selection made.

Sum of SALES	Column Labels		
Row Labels	2014	2015	Grand Total
EAST	2,000,000	57,650	2,057,650
NORTH	1,000,000	63,116	1,063,116
SOUTH	1,500,000	38,281	1,538,281
WEST	2,500,000	90,967	2,590,967
Grand Total	7,000,000	250,014	7,250,014

Format Error Values

There are times when you will receive errors in a pivot table if you include a formula or a calculated item. This error will look ugly, especially when you are presenting the analysis to a lot of people. It is easy to override this error by including a default value that should be used instead of the error.

Step One: If you look at the pivot table below, you will notice that there is an error in the calculation for one record.

Sum of SALES	Column Labels		
Row Labels	2014	2015	Change
EAST	4,131,596	3,625,352	-12%
NORTH	0	1,540,521	#DIV/0!
SOUTH	2,226,079	4,040,499	82%
WEST	4,922,643	4,738,291	-4%

Step Two: Right click on a cell in the pivot table and go to the option 'Pivot table Options.'

CUSTOMER	REGION	ORDER DATE	SALES	MONTH	YEAR
Acme, inc.	NORTH	13/04/2014			2014
Widget Corp	SOUTH	21/12/2014	$2,2		2014
123 Warehousing	EAST	15/02/2014	$4,1		2014
Demo Company	WEST	14/05/2014	$4,9		2014
Smith and Co.	NORTH	28/06/2015	$1,5		2015
Foo Bars	SOUTH	15/01/2015	$4,0		2015
ABC Telecom	EAST	22/08/2015	$3,6		2015
Fake Brothers	WEST	31/12/2015	$4,7		2015

Right-click context menu items:
- Copy
- Format Cells...
- Number Format...
- Refresh
- Sort ▶
- Move
- ✕ Remove 'Sum of SALES'
- Summarize Values By ▶
- Show Values As ▶
- Show Details
- Show/Hide Fields ▶
- Value Field Settings...
- PivotTable Options...
- Hide Field List
- Show PivotPal

Sum of SALES	Column Labels ▾		
Row Labels ▾	2014	2015	C
EAST	4,131,596	3,625,352	
NORTH	0	1,540,521	#DIV/0!
SOUTH	2,226,079	4,040,499	
WEST	4,922,643	4,738,291	

Calibri ▾ 11 ▾ A A ▾ % ▾
B I ☰ ▾ A ▾ ▾

Step Three: Select the option 'For Error Values Show' in the dialog box that is open on your screen.

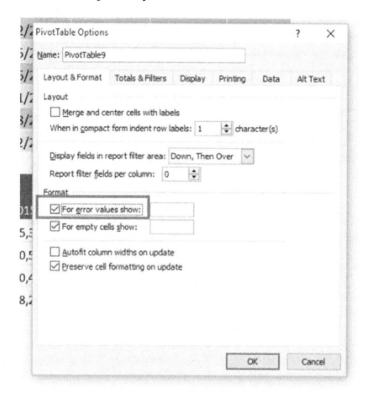

Step Four: Now, enter any value or text in the box.

The error values in the pivot table are not formatted properly.

Sum of SALES	Column Labels		
Row Labels	2014	2015	Change
EAST	4,131,596	3,625,352	-12%
NORTH	0	1,540,521	na
SOUTH	2,226,079	4,040,499	82%
WEST	4,922,643	4,738,291	-4%

Format Empty Cells

There are many times when you may have created a pivot table that has numerous empty cells values. You would have been worried about what exactly is happening in Excel. The only reason there are blanks in the pivot table is that there are some blank cells in the data source. This does happen occasionally, especially if you are downloading your source data from the Internet. You can fix this issue in your pivot table by using a default value for the missing data in the source data.

Step One: There is no data in the pivot table below for the North label. Let us now see how this can be changed.

Row Labels	Sum of SALES
EAST	2,057,650
NORTH	
SOUTH	1,538,281
WEST	2,590,967
Grand Total	6,186,898

Step Two: Go to the Pivot Table tools section in the menu bar, and click the 'Options' button. A dialog box will open.

Step Three: You should now set the default value for the empty cells in the source data.

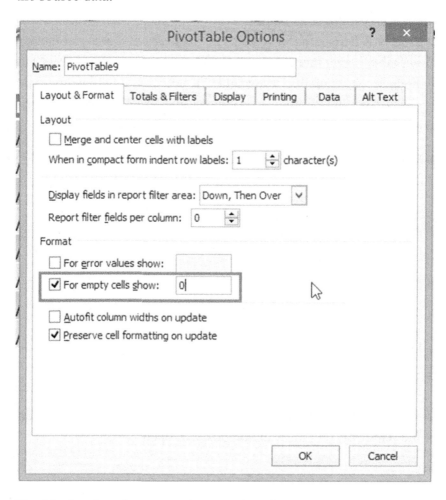

The blank values have now been replaced.

Row Labels	Sum of SALES
EAST	2,057,650
NORTH	0
SOUTH	1,538,281
WEST	2,590,967
Grand Total	**6,186,898**

Keep Column Widths Constant

When you refresh a pivot table, you will notice that the columns automatically change in width depending on the content present in the column. This is annoying since you would have spent a sufficient amount of time to align the columns. You do not have to worry about this, since you can use the Pivot Table options to fix this issue. When you update the source data and then refresh the pivot table, you will notice that the width of the column does not change.

Step one: Right click on any cell in the pivot table and choose 'Pivot table Options.'

Sum of SALES	Column Labels		
Row Labels	2014	2015	
EAST	485,772	346,513	
NORTH	387,082	386,462	
SOUTH	331,581	403,764	
WEST	100,173	292,243	
Grand Total	1,304,608	1,428,98	

Copy
Format Cells...
Refresh
Move
Show/Hide Fields
PivotTable Options...
Hide Field List
Show PivotPal

Step Two: Uncheck the option to auto fit the column width when you update the pivot table.

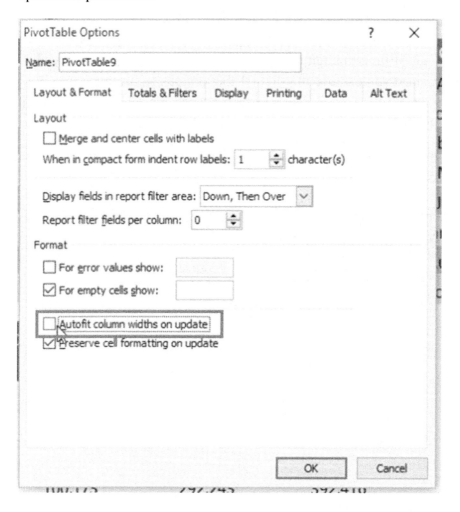

Step Three: Now, update the data in the source.

CUSTOMER	REGION	ORDER DATE	SALES	MONTH	YEAR
Acme, inc.	NORTH	13/04/2014	$387,082	April	2014
Widget Corp	SOUTH	21/12/2014	$331,581	December	2014
23 Warehousir	EAST	15/02/2014	568∰44	February	2014
Demo Company	WEST	14/05/2014	$100,173	May	2014
Smith and Co.	NORTH	28/06/2015	$386,462	June	2015
Foo Bars	SOUTH	15/01/2015	$403,764	January	2015

Step Four: Refresh the pivot table.

Sum of SALES	Column Labels ▾		
Row Labels ▾	2014	201	📋 Copy
			✎ Format Cells...
EAST	485,772	346,5	📄 Refresh
NORTH	387,082	386,4	Move ▸
SOUTH	331,581	403,7	Show/Hide Fields ▸
WEST	100,173	292,2	PivotTable Options...
			📋 Show Field List
Grand Total	1,304,608	1,428,	Show PivotPal

The width of your pivot table will no longer change.

Sum of SALES	Column Labels ▾		
Row Labels ▾	2014	2015	Grand Total
EAST	568,444	346,513	914,957
NORTH	387,082	386,462	773,544
SOUTH	331,581	403,764	735,345
WEST	100,173	292,243	392,416
Grand Total	1,387,280	1,428,982	2,816,262

Showing the Report Filters on Multiple Sheets

You can always show the items that are present in the Report Filter in different sheets in your workbook. Let us assume that you have a pivot table that will show the user the number of transactions and the total sales made by a customer. You should first remove the customer field from the report filter and save the pivot table. Copy this table in a separate sheet for every customer. Every customer in the data will have a different pivot table in a separate sheet. This pivot table will contain the transactional metrics and the individual sales for every customer. This is how the pivot table we will be using in this example looks like:

CUSTOMER	REGION	ORDER DATE	SALES	MONTH	YEAR
Acme, inc.	NORTH	13/04/2014	$1,000,000	April	2014
Widget Corp	SOUTH	21/12/2014	$1,500,000	December	2014
123 Warehousing	EAST	15/02/2014	$2,000,000	February	2014
Demo Company	WEST	14/05/2014	$2,500,000	May	2014
Smith and Co.	NORTH	28/06/2015	$63,116	June	2015
Foo Bars	SOUTH	15/01/2015	$38,281	January	2015

Row Labels	Sum of SALES	Count of SALES2
EAST	2,000,000	1
NORTH	1,063,116	2
SOUTH	1,538,281	2
WEST	2,500,000	1
Grand Total	7,101,397	6

Step One: Now, remove the customer field from the report section of the pivot table area.

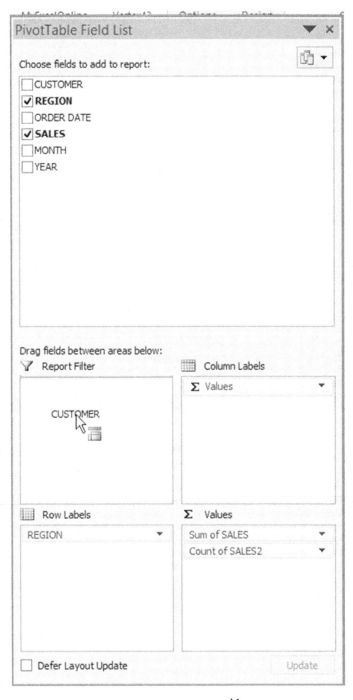

Step Two: Now, move to the Options Tab and click on the drop down arrow. Choose the option to Show Report Filter Pages.

Step Three: Now, click OK.

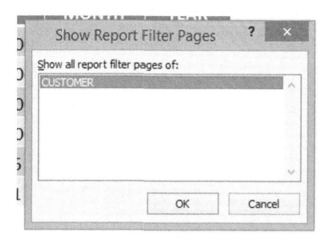

You will now see that the pivot table for every customer will appear on a new sheet.

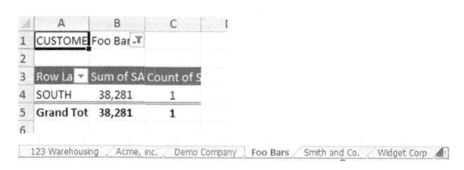

Average

You can choose different calculations that you can perform on the source data by choosing a specific operation in the Summarize Values By window. You can calculate the sum, count, average, maximum, minimum, etc.

When you add a numeric value into the Values Area in the pivot table pane, Excel will automatically calculate the sum of those values. It is easy for you to convert this calculation from a sum into the average. This will give you the mean or average value for the values in the source data.

Step One: Now, click the source data and go to the Insert tab in the menu bar. Select Insert Pivot table.

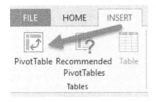

Step Two: When you do this, you will see the Create Pivot Table box on your screen. Excel will automatically select the range of the table or source data. You can choose to insert the pivot table in the existing worksheet or in a new worksheet.

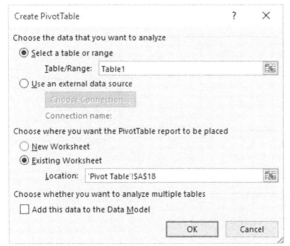

Step Four: Now, drag and drop the required fields into the pivot tables pane in your excel workbook.

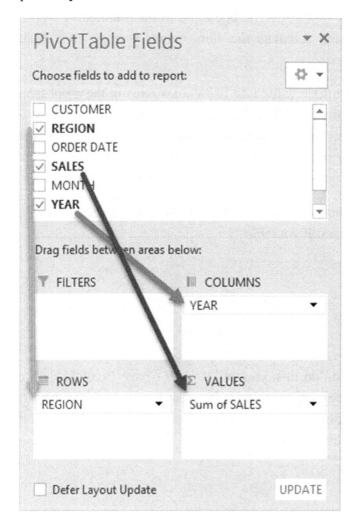

Step Five: Once your pivot table is set up, you can select any value in the pivot table and right click on the cell. Now, choose to summarize the values in the pivot based on the average.

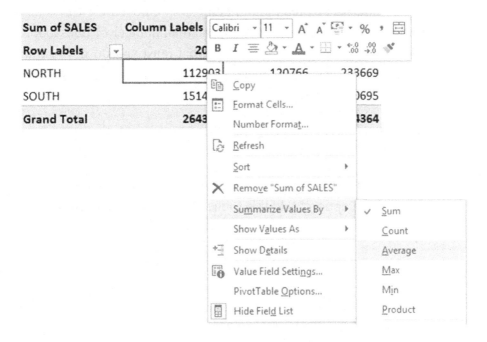

Step Six: You now have a pivot table report that will show you the average sales for the region in one year.

Average of SALES	Column Labels		
Row Labels	2014	2015	Grand Total
NORTH	56451.5	60383	58417.25
SOUTH	75723.5	64624	70173.75
Grand Total	66087.5	62503.5	64295.5

Calculates a Unique Count

The developers at Microsoft are adding new features to Excel in every edition that they release, and some new features are overdue. In the previous section, we created a pivot table, and removed the Customers field from the row labels, and obtained the total number of transactions that were performed the customers. So, what must you do if you want to show the total for each customer? You can do this in a pivot table by using the Data Model option.

Step One: Insert a pivot table for the source data that you have obtained.

Step Two: In the dialog box that opens, ensure that you check the button against the option 'Add this to the Data model' and click OK.

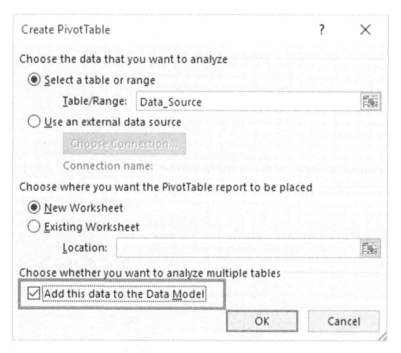

Step Three: You will now see a pivot table on your screen. Remove the customer field from both the row and values areas. This will give you a total transaction value for every customer in the source data.

Step Four: If you want to obtain a distinct count of the variables in the source data, you should click on Customers in the values area of the pivot pane. Click on the drop down arrow and select the 'Value Field Settings' option.

Step Five: You should select the 'Distinct Count' option from the list in the dialog box, and click OK.

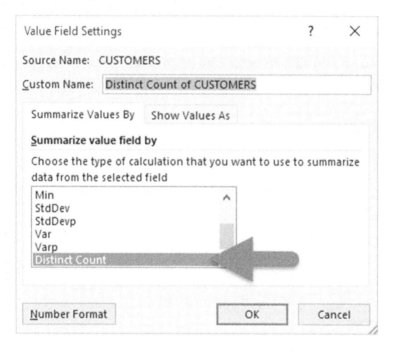

Percent Of grand Total

An Excel pivot table allows you to perform numerous calculations, and the percent of grand total is one such calculation that it can perform. Excel will automatically calculate the percentage values for you using the numbers present in the column. Remember that this is only done when the values in the columns are all numbers. The example below looks at how you can calculate the percentage of the grand total of the values in any column.

Step One: You should first insert a new pivot table in the excel sheet with the data.

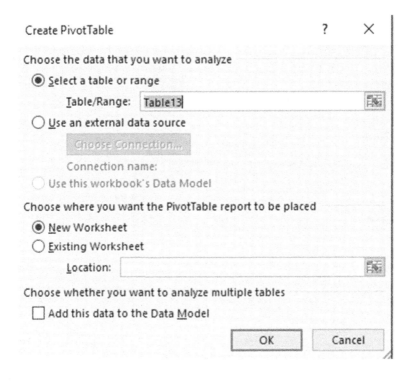

Step Two: You should add the Sales month field to the rows section, the financial year to the columns section and include the sales value twice in the Values area of the pivot table pane.

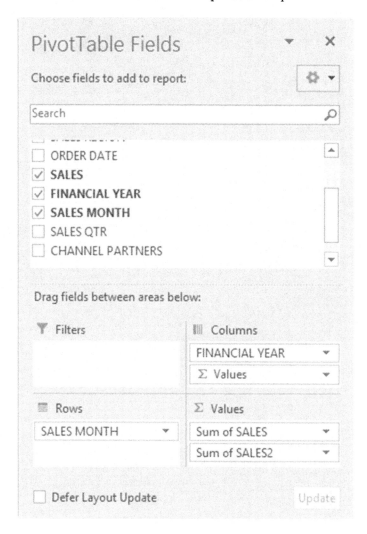

Step Three: You should now choose the second sales field, and click the drop down arrow. Choose the 'Value Field Settings' option from the window that opens.

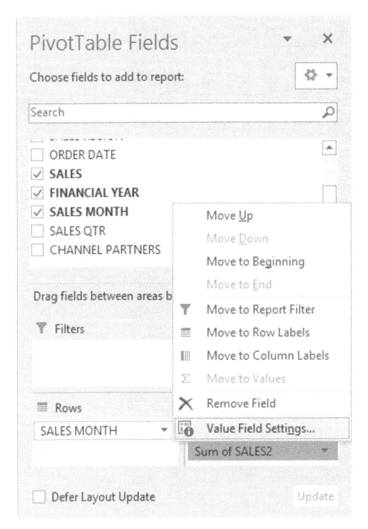

Step Four: Now, select the "Show Values As" tab. Click on the drop down arrow and choose the percent of grand total. You should also change the name of the column from Custom name to Percent of Grand Total. This will make the pivot more presentable.

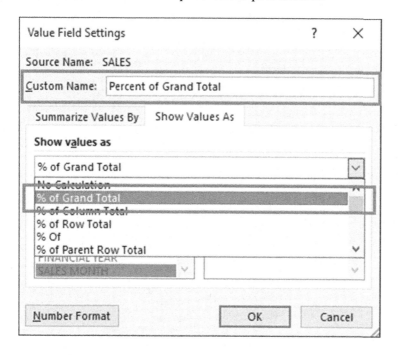

Step Five: If you notice clearly, you will see that the data is now in a decimal format that is very hard for any user to read.

Column Labels		
	2012	
Row Labels	Sum of SALES	Percent of Grand Total
January	771186	0.02
February	867220	0.03
March	784136	0.02
April	908666	0.03
May	893039	0.03
June	786918	0.02
July	1056573	0.03
August	806719	0.03
September	863089	0.03
October	873208	0.03
November	923402	0.03
December	854090	0.03
Grand Total	10388246	0.32

If you want to format the column labeled Percent of Grand Total, you should click on the percent of grand total column (also the second sales field). Click on the drop down arrow, and select 'Value Field Settings.' You must transform the numbers from the decimal format into a more readable format.

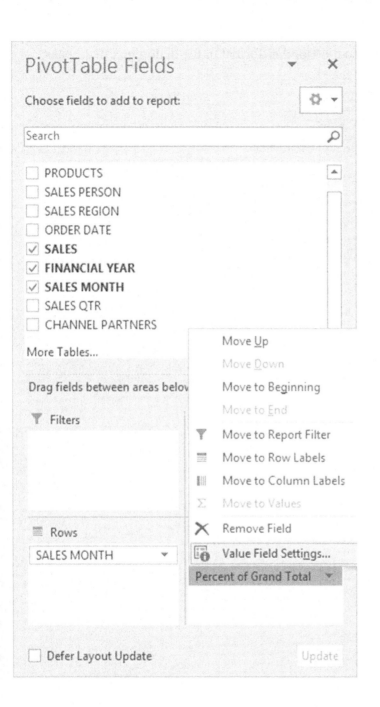

Step Six: Choose the Number format in the dialog box that opens.

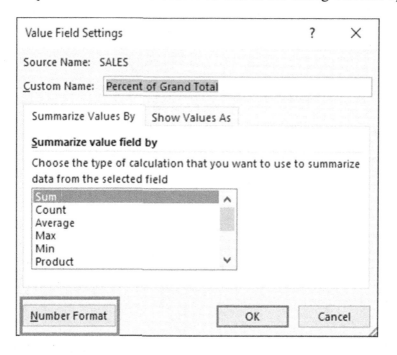

Step Seven: You should make the changes to the formatting in the Format cells dialog box. Click OK twice. For the purpose of this example, we will be using the percentage category to make it easier for users to read the percentage values of the grand total.

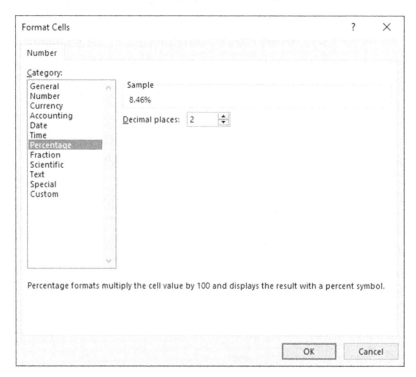

Excel will now create the pivot table. This table will show you the percentage of the grand total for the information across different years. The sales numbers are always represented as the percentage of the grand total. If you look at the image below, you will note that the figure is represented as a percentage.

Row Labels	Sum of SALES (2012)	Percent of Grand Total (2012)	Sum of SALES (2013)	Percent of Grand Total (2013)	Sum of SALES (2014)	Percent of Grand Total (2014)	Total Sum of SALES	Total Percent of Grand Total
January	771186	2.41%	872080	2.72%	1074820	3.35%	2718086	8.48%
February	867220	2.70%	909654	2.84%	807257	2.52%	2584131	8.06%
March	784136	2.45%	1031596	3.22%	1013466	3.16%	2829198	8.82%
April	908666	2.83%	968855	3.02%	836559	2.61%	2714080	8.46%
May	893039	2.79%	850502	2.65%	791095	2.47%	2534636	7.90%
June	786918	2.45%	981050	3.06%	771976	2.41%	2539944	7.92%
July	1056573	3.30%	854835	2.67%	873543	2.72%	2784951	8.69%
August	806719	2.52%	1002597	3.13%	599246	1.87%	2408562	7.51%
September	863089	2.69%	814513	2.54%	1011288	3.15%	2688890	8.39%
October	873208	2.72%	931193	2.90%	1059308	3.30%	2863709	8.93%
November	923402	2.88%	769352	2.40%	812659	2.53%	2505413	7.81%
December	854090	2.66%	1031897	3.22%	1006745	3.14%	2892732	9.02%
Grand Total	10388246	32.40%	11018124	34.36%	10657962	33.24%	32064332	100.00%

Percentage of Column Total

An Excel pivot table will have numerous calculations under the "Show Values As" option, and the Percent of Column Total is one calculation that can help you the most. You can calculate the percentage values for the pivot using this option. You will notice that the pivot table will calculate the percentage of any value that is present in the source data in an instant. We will look at how we can calculate the percent of column total in a pivot table in the sections below.

Step One: Now, click on the data and insert a new pivot table. To do this, go to the Insert tab, select Pivot table and choose to create the table either in a new worksheet or in the existing worksheet.

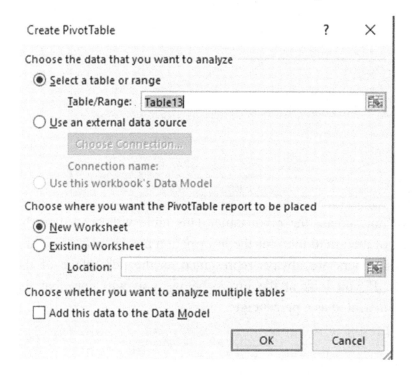

Step Two: In the rows section in the pivot pane, add the sales month field. Add the financial year field to the columns area and add the sales field twice in the values area of the pivot table pane. We will look at why we are doing this in the sections below.

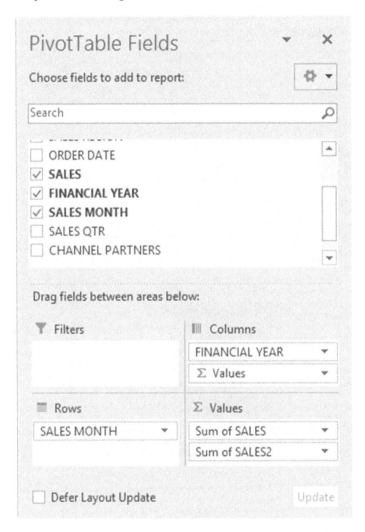

Step Three: Now, move to the second sum of sales field column, and click on the drop down arrow. Open the Value Field Settings option.

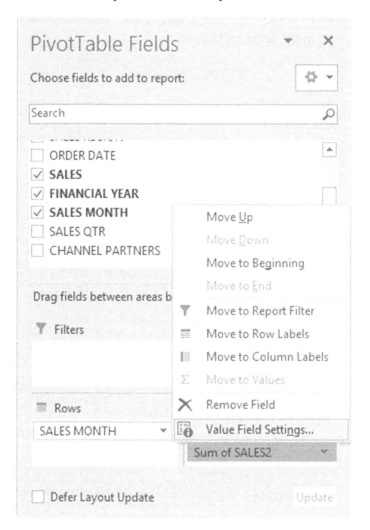

Step Four: Choose the Show Values As option, and click on the drop down arrow. Select the % Column Total. You can also change the name of the column to Percent of Column Total. This will make the pivot table more presentable. Click OK.

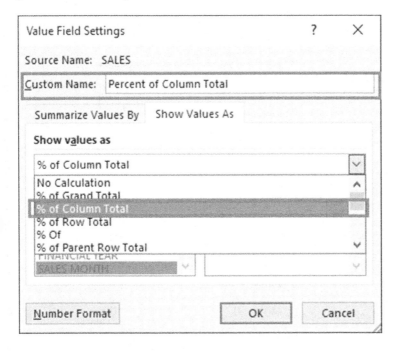

Step Five: If you look carefully at the screen below, you will find it hard to read the decimal format in the column 'Percent of Column Total.'

2012		
Row Labels ▾	Sum of SALES	Percent of Column Total
January	771186	0.07
February	867220	0.08
March	784136	0.08
April	908666	0.09
May	893039	0.09
June	786918	0.08
July	1056573	0.10
August	806719	0.08
September	863089	0.08
October	873208	0.08
November	923402	0.09
December	854090	0.08
Grand Total	10388246	1.00

You can also format the column 'Percent of Column Total.' To do this, you should click on the drop down near the percent of column total column, and choose the option 'Value Field Settings.' The objective is to transform the numbers in that column into a percentage from the decimal format. This will make it easier for people to read the number.

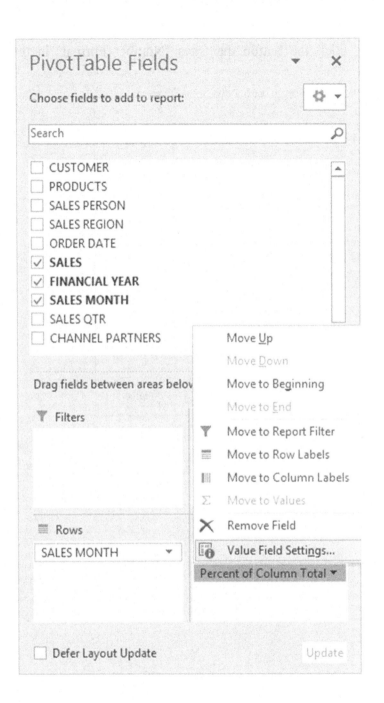

PivotTable Fields

Choose fields to add to report:

Search 🔍

- ☐ CUSTOMER
- ☐ PRODUCTS
- ☐ SALES PERSON
- ☐ SALES REGION
- ☐ ORDER DATE
- ☑ **SALES**
- ☑ **FINANCIAL YEAR**
- ☑ **SALES MONTH**
- ☐ SALES QTR
- ☐ CHANNEL PARTNERS

Drag fields between areas belov

▼ Filters

▤ Rows

| SALES MONTH ▼ |

	Move Up
	Move Down
	Move to Beginning
	Move to End
▼	Move to Report Filter
▤	Move to Row Labels
▥	Move to Column Labels
Σ	Move to Values
✕	Remove Field
🗗	Value Field Settings...

Percent of Column Total ▼

☐ Defer Layout Update   Update

Step Six: Now, click the button that says 'Number Format' in the dialog box.

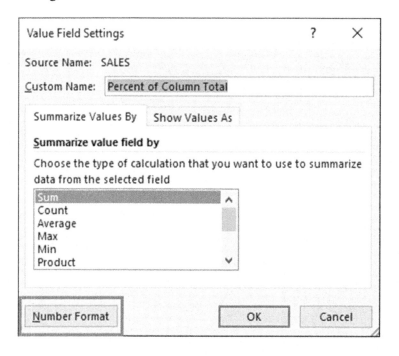

Step Seven: You can make the changes to the formatting inside the format cells dialog box, and click on Ok twice. In this section, we are using the percentage category to calculate the percentage values to obtain the percent of the column total values. This makes it easier for any external user to read the numbers.

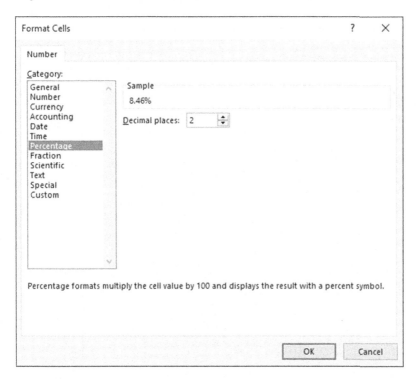

The pivot table on your screen will now show the percentage of the column total across different years. The sales numbers are all represented as the percentage of the total of each column. You will see that this column is represented as a total of one hundred percent.

Row Labels	Sum of SALES	Percent of Column Total	Sum of SALES	Percent of Column Total	Sum of SALES	Percent of Column Total	Total Sum of SALES	Total Percent of Column Total
		2012		2013		2014		
January	771186	7.42%	872080	7.91%	1074820	10.08%	2718086	8.48%
February	867220	8.35%	909654	8.26%	807257	7.57%	2584131	8.06%
March	784136	7.55%	1031596	9.36%	1013466	9.51%	2829198	8.82%
April	903666	8.75%	968855	8.79%	836559	7.85%	2714080	8.46%
May	893039	8.60%	850502	7.72%	791095	7.42%	2534636	7.90%
June	786918	7.58%	981050	8.90%	771976	7.24%	2539944	7.92%
July	1056573	10.17%	854835	7.76%	873543	8.20%	2784951	8.69%
August	806719	7.77%	1002597	9.10%	599246	5.62%	2408562	7.51%
September	863089	8.31%	814513	7.39%	1011288	9.49%	2688890	8.39%
October	873208	8.41%	931193	8.45%	1059308	9.94%	2863709	8.93%
November	923402	8.89%	769352	6.98%	812659	7.62%	2505413	7.81%
December	854090	8.22%	1031897	9.37%	1006745	9.45%	2892732	9.02%
Grand Total	10388246	100.00%	11018124	100.00%	10657962	100.00%	32064332	100.00%

Percentage of Row Total

The percent of row total is similar to the percent of column total. Excel will automatically calculate the percentage of the values if there are numbers in your source data. In this section, we will look at how to obtain the percentage of the row total.

Step One: Insert a new pivot table for the source data.

Step Two: Add the Sales person to the rows section of the pivot table, the financial year field to the columns table and the sales field in the values area. You should add the sales field to the value area twice.

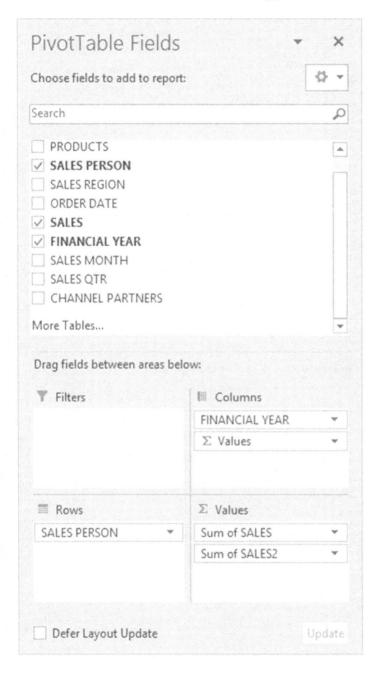

Step Three: Click the drop down arrow near the header 'Sum of Sales2,' and choose the Value Field Settings option in the window that opens.

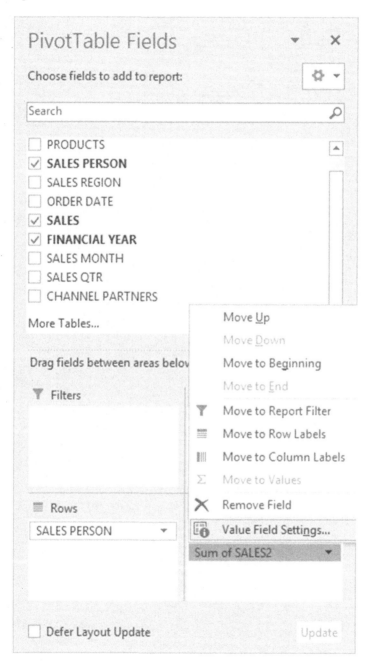

Step Four: You should now select the 'Show Values As' tab and select the '% of Row Total' option. You should also change the custom name to make the data in the pivot more presentable.

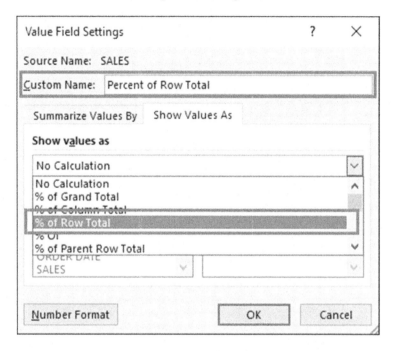

Step Five: The information in the new column in the pivot will be hard to read since the numbers are in a decimal format.

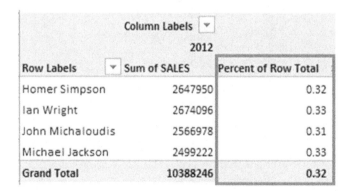

You should click on the percent of row total column, and click the drop down arrow. Now, choose the 'Value Field Settings' option from the window that opens. Select the percentage option since you want to convert the format to percentage from decimal to improve readability.

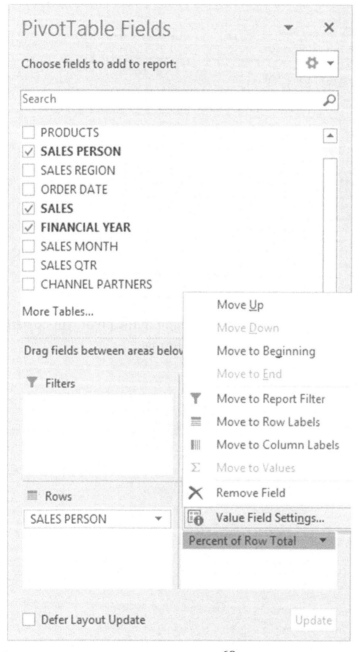

Step Six: Now, choose the number format button.

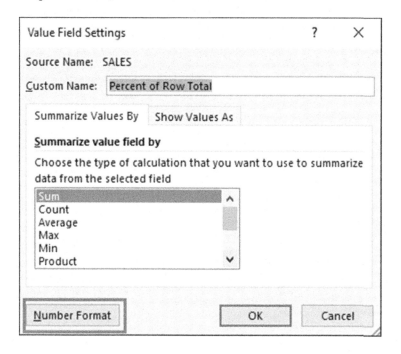

Value Field Settings   ?   ✕

Source Name: SALES

Custom Name: Percent of Row Total

Summarize Values By   Show Values As

Summarize value field by

Choose the type of calculation that you want to use to summarize
data from the selected field

| Sum |
| Count |
| Average |
| Max |
| Min |
| Product |

Number Format   OK   Cancel

Step Seven: You can make some changes to the format in the pivot within the Format Cells box and click OK. In the example below, we will be using the percentage category to make it easier for a user to read the numbers.

You will now see the Percent of Row Total for the sales data across the years in the updated pivot. The sales numbers in the pivot will now be represented as a percentage of every row in the source data.

Row Labels	Sum of SALES	2012 Percent of Row Total	Sum of SALES	2013 Percent of Row Total	Sum of SALES	2014 Percent of Row Total	Total Sum of SALES	Total Percent of Row Total
Homer Simpson	2647950	31.76%	2987445	35.83%	2701418	32.40%	8336813	100.00%
Ian Wright	2674096	33.13%	2722129	33.72%	2675496	33.15%	8071721	100.00%
John Michaloudis	2566978	31.47%	2879900	35.30%	2711156	33.23%	8158034	100.00%
Michael Jackson	2499222	33.33%	2428650	32.39%	2569892	34.28%	7497764	100.00%
Grand Total	10388246	32.40%	11018124	34.36%	10657962	33.24%	32064332	100.00%

Variance Calculations

You can perform numerous calculations in an Excel pivot table using the "Show Values As" option. The option that is often used is the Difference From calculation. You can always use the base period as days, weeks, months, years, etc. It is a good idea to use this option when your manager asks you how your company is doing when compared to the past. The example below will show you how you can look at the variance from the previous year.

Step One: Insert a pivot chart for the source data.

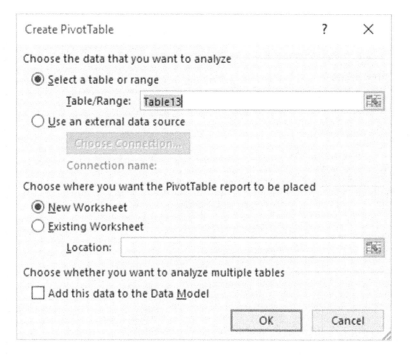

Step Two: In the Rows area of the pivot, add the Months field, add the years field to the columns area and the sales field twice to the values area.

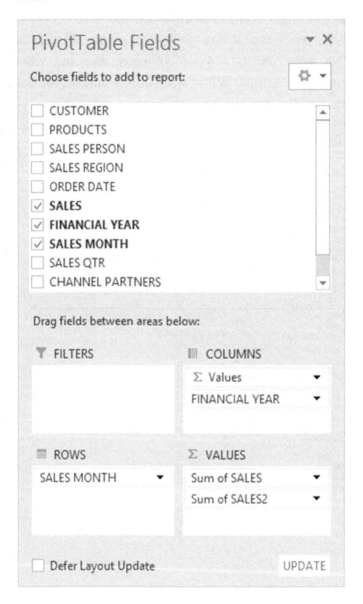

Step Three: Now, select the second sales field in the options below and click the drop down arrow. Choose the Value Field Settings.

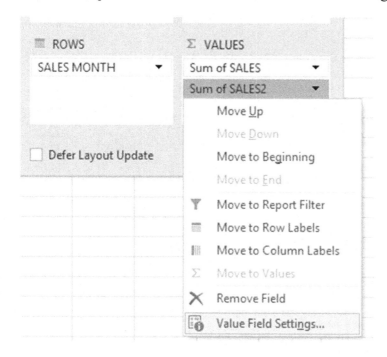

Step Four: You should then select the Show values As Tab, and click on the drop down. Choose the option 'Difference From' in the window that appears.

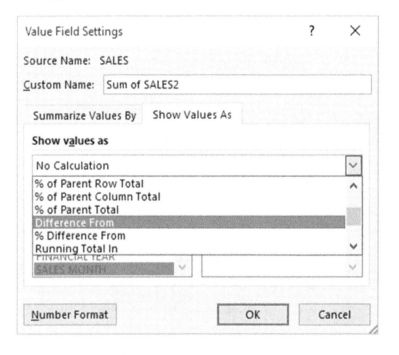

Step Five: You will now need to choose the base items. You can choose the previous financial year and click OK. The header in the pivot table will now read 'Difference from the previous Financial Year.'

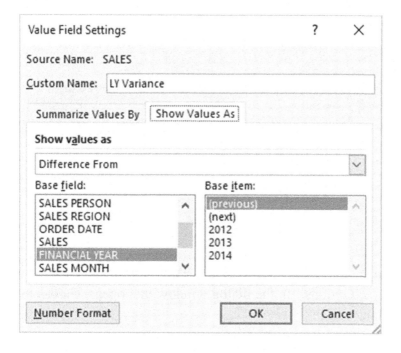

Step Six: If you want to format the values of the pivot table, you should go to the PivotTable Tools option, select 'Analyze/Options' and then select the entire pivot table.

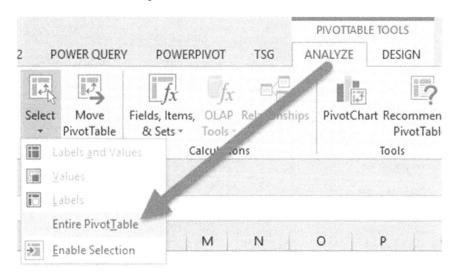

You will then need to go to the PivotTable Tools option and choose the option 'Analyze/Options.' In the dialog window that opens, choose the 'Values' option.

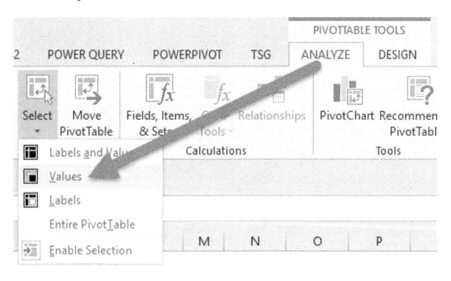

If you want to open the format cells dialog box in the pivot table, click on the shortcut Ctrl+1. You can make the necessary formatting changes and hit OK. Remember that this will change the format of the entire column, and if you add any new field to the pivot table, it will take the same format.

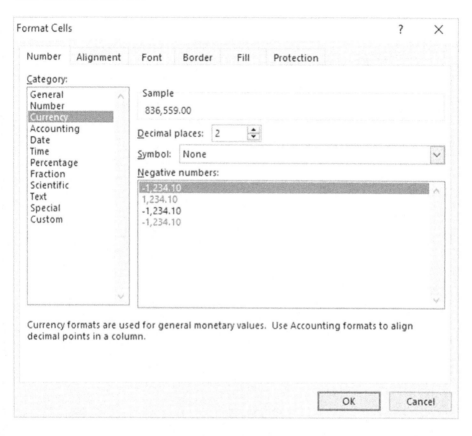

Step Seven: If you want to change the name of the header within a pivot table, all you need to do is click on that header and manually make the adjustments.

Row Labels ▾	Column Labe ▾		
	2012	2013	
	Sum of SALES	Sum of SALES	LY Var
January	771,186	872,080	100,894
February	867,220	909,654	42,434

Step Eight: You must first select the entire column that contains the empty values and hide them. Remember that you should select the entire column to do this.

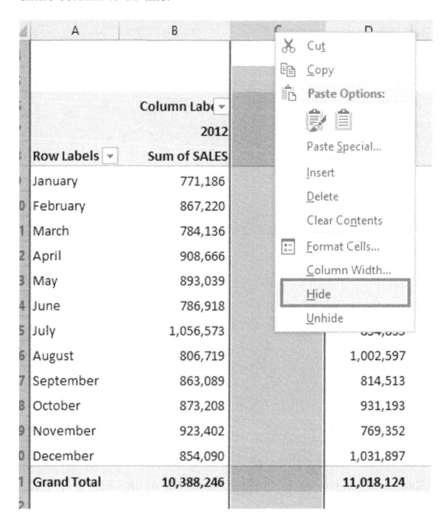

Row Labels ▾	Column Labe ▾ 2012 Sum of SALES		
January	771,186		
February	867,220		
March	784,136		
April	908,666		
May	893,039		
June	786,918		
July	1,056,573		
August	806,719	1,002,597
September	863,089	814,513
October	873,208	931,193
November	923,402	769,352
December	854,090	1,031,897
Grand Total	10,388,246	11,018,124

You will now see that the pivot table that you have created is formatted fully, and shows the difference or variance in the figures when compared to the previous year.

	Column Lab(▾				
	2012	2013		2014	
Row Labels ▾	Sum of SALES	Sum of SALES	LY Variance	Sum of SALES	LY Variance
January	771,186	872,080	100,894	1,074,820	202,740
February	867,220	909,654	42,434	807,257	-102,397
March	784,136	1,031,596	247,460	1,013,466	-18,130
April	908,666	968,855	60,189	836,559	-132,296
May	893,039	850,502	-42,537	791,095	-59,407
June	786,918	981,050	194,132	771,976	-209,074
July	1,056,573	854,835	-201,738	873,543	18,708
August	806,719	1,002,597	195,878	599,246	-403,351
September	863,089	814,513	-48,576	1,011,288	196,775
October	873,208	931,193	57,985	1,059,308	128,115
November	923,402	769,352	-154,050	812,659	43,307
December	854,090	1,031,897	177,807	1,006,745	-25,152
Grand Total	10,388,246	11,018,124	629,878	10,657,962	-360,162

Running Total In

A running total is a value that accumulates the data across a certain period like weeks, months, years or even days. This option is also known as the year to date analysis. This value will take the value of one period; add that value to the second period, then the third period and so on to give you the accumulated value. If you are well versed with statistics, you will know that this is called a cumulative value. You can either show this value in the percentage form or the currency form. You do not have to include a formula or multiple functions to calculate this in Excel.

Step One: You should first insert a pivot table for your source data.

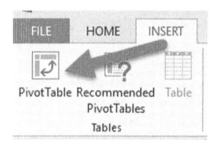

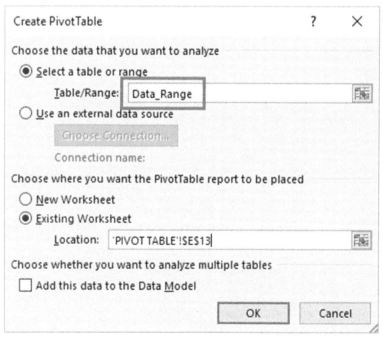

Step Two: Now, add the month's field to the rows area, the year field to the column area and add the sales field to the values area. Make sure that you add the sales field twice to the values area as you did earlier.

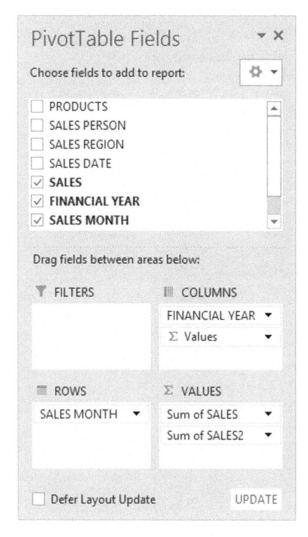

Step Three: Now, right click on any of the total cells and remove the grand total.

	Column Labels ▾				
	2015		Total Sum of SALES	Total Su...	
Row Labels ▾	Sum of SALES	Sum of SALES2			
January	148974	148974	148974		
February	117520	117520	117520		
March	103332	103332	103332		
April	412722	412722	412722		
May	318824	318824	318824		
June	201099	201099	201099		
July	163269	163269	163269		
August	505220	505220	505220		
September	1245609	1245609	1245609		1245609
October	1119150	1119150	1119150		1119150
November	979177	979177	979177		979177

B I ≡ ◇ ▾ A ▾ ⊞ ▾

- Copy
- Format Cells...
- Number Format...
- Refresh
- Remove Grand Total
- Summarize Values By ▸
- Value Field Settings...
- PivotTable Options...
- Hide Field List

Step Four: Now, move to the header 'Sum of Sales2' and click on the drop down arrow. In the window that appears, click on Show Values As. You can then choose the option % running total in and choose the base field as months.

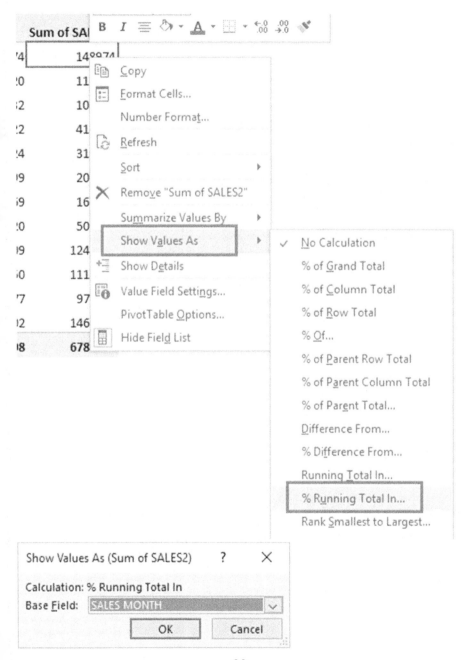

Step Five: Now, you can manually update the name of the second sum field. This can be done by clicking on the title in the pivot table.

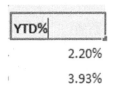

2.20%

3.93%

Step Six: You can now insert a pivot chart on the screen. This can be done by going to PivotTable Tools, clicking on Options/Analyze and choosing the Pivot Chart option.

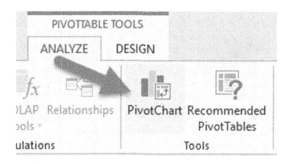

Step Seven: Select the Combo Chart option in the Insert Chart dialog box. Now, select the YTD% series as the secondary axis and click OK.

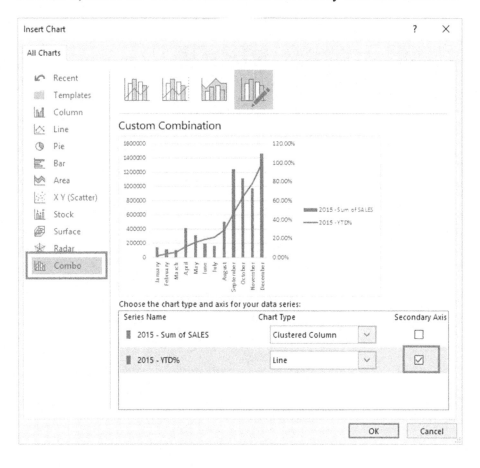

Now, the percentage of the totals are shown in the pivot table, and these are also shown in the form of a graph using the pivot chart option.

Row Labels	Column Labels 2015 Sum of SALES	YTD%
January	148974	2.20%
February	117520	3.93%
March	103332	5.45%
April	412722	11.54%
May	318824	16.24%
June	201099	19.20%
July	163269	21.61%
August	505220	29.06%
September	1245609	47.42%
October	1119150	63.92%
November	979177	78.36%
December	1468002	100.00%
Grand Total	**6782898**	

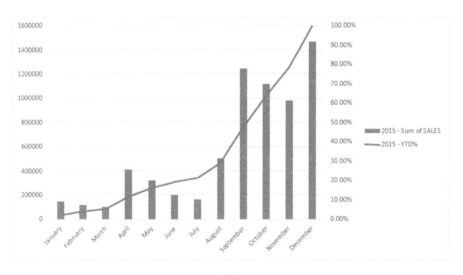

Group by Date

It is easy to group the data in a pivot table on the basis of the dates. You should move to the Dates column in the pivot table, and right click on any cell in the column. Now, choose the option to group the data based on the dates. A dialog box will open which will allow you to group the data in the pivot table based on the days, months, quarters and years.

Step One: move to the "dates" column in the pivot, and right click on the cell. Now, select the option 'Group…' from the window.

Step Two: Now, select the right combination and group the data in the right format. Now, click OK.

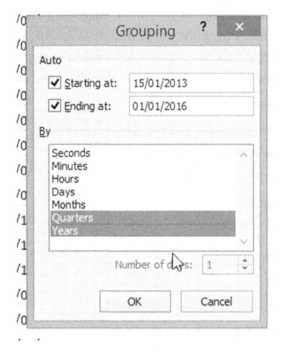

The pivot table on the screen is now grouped by the dates.

Sum of SALES	Column Labels				
Row Labels	EAST	NORTH	SOUTH	WEST	Grand Total
⊟ 2013					
Qtr1	44,802	26,884	46,174		117,860
Qtr2		80,369	53,522	49,049	182,940
Qtr3	67,320	58,146		66,663	192,129
Qtr4	22,024		83,288	64,750	170,062
⊟ 2014					
Qtr1	29,570	53,586	14,333		97,489
Qtr2		25,263	68,797	83,468	177,528
Qtr3	49,562	23,798		13,964	87,324
Qtr4	78,715		16,843	80,780	176,338
⊟ 2015					
Qtr1	37,544	56,959	47,189		141,692
Qtr2		20,816	85,607	53,413	159,836
Qtr3	Sum of SALES	56,959		43,216	114,834
Qtr4	Value: No value	20,816	47,189	53,413	158,962
Grand Total	Row: 2015 - Qtr2				
	Column: EAST	423.596	462.942	508.716	1.776.994

89

Group By years and quarters

Have you ever needed to report the sales data based on quarters or years? What would you do if you only had daily sales data? You will need to group the data using some complex formulae. A pivot table makes this process easier, and you will not make any errors either. This will make it easier for you to update the report using any additional data. The example below will show you how you can group the data based on the quarters and years.

Step One: Insert a pivot table.

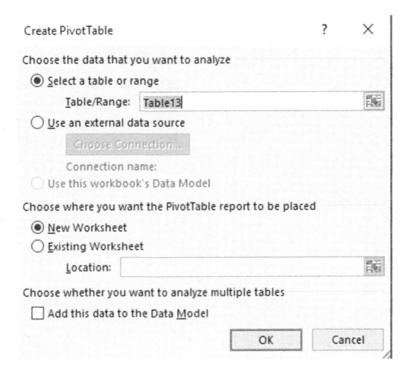

Step Two: Select the 'Order Date' field in the rows section in the pivot table pane. The latest versions of Excel will group the data automatically based on the years and quarters.

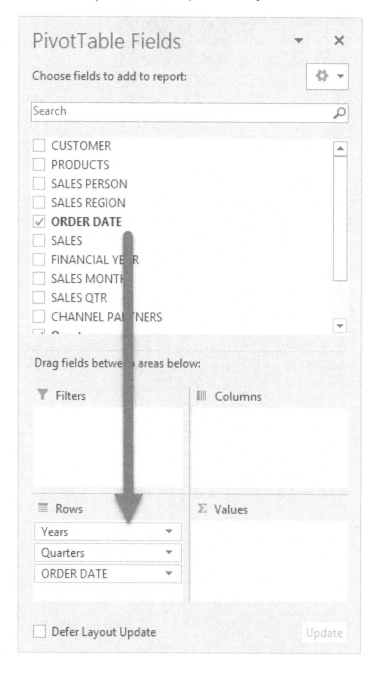

Step Three: If you are using an older version of Excel, right click on any value in the pivot table and select the 'Group' option.

Step Four: Excel is smart to determine the data range that you want to use to group the data. You must ensure that you only select the quarters and years. These will be highlighted in blue. This will instruct excel to group the data based on quarters and years.

You will notice that the year's field has been added to the pivot table field list automatically. This field can now be used in different pivot table analyses.

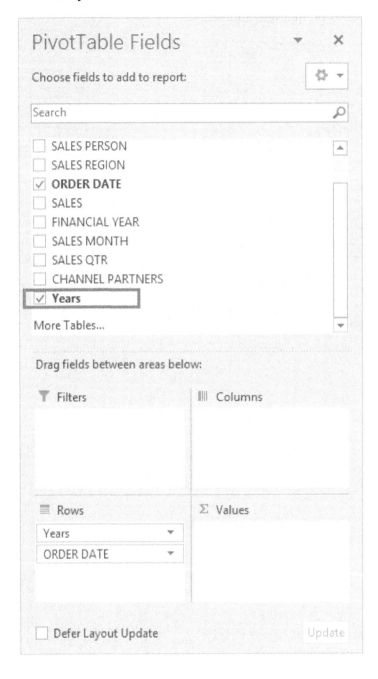

Step Five: Add the Sales field to the values area in the pivot table pane, and obtain the sales for every range.

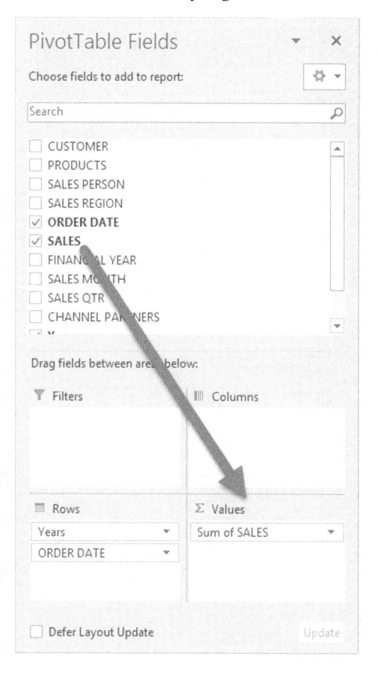

You will now see that the values have been grouped by the years and quarters. You can always improve the formatting of the data.

	A	B
4		
5		
6	Row Labels ▼	Sum of SALES
7	⊟ 2012	
8	Qtr1	1322504
9	Qtr2	1676623
10	Qtr3	2850375
11	Qtr4	4538744
12	⊟ 2013	
13	Qtr1	1523771
14	Qtr2	3547993
15	Qtr3	2380031
16	Qtr4	3566329
17	⊟ 2014	
18	Qtr1	1148861
19	Qtr2	3126441
20	Qtr3	2021263
21	Qtr4	4361397
22	Grand Total	32064332
23		

Step Six: Now choose the sum of sales, and select the option 'Value Field Settings.'

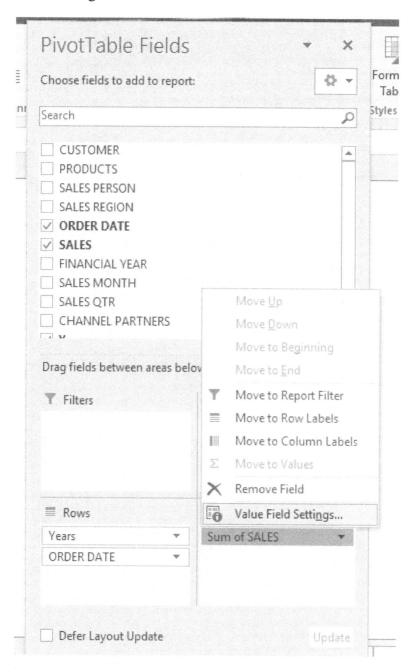

Step Seven: Choose the number format.

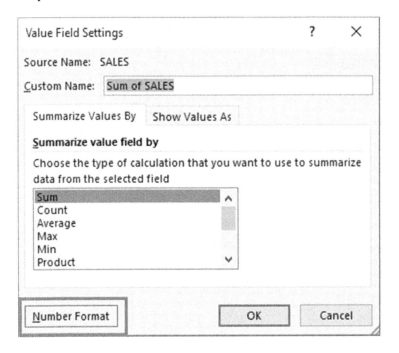

Step Eight: Choose the option 'Currency' in the dialog box and click OK.

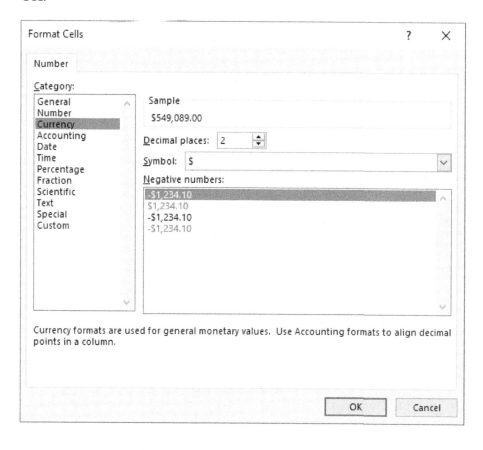

You will now see that you have the total sales value for every quarter.

Row Labels	Sum of SALES
⊖ 2012	
Qtr1	$1,322,504.00
Qtr2	$1,676,623.00
Qtr3	$2,850,375.00
Qtr4	$4,538,744.00
⊖ 2013	
Qtr1	$1,523,771.00
Qtr2	$3,547,993.00
Qtr3	$2,380,031.00
Qtr4	$3,566,329.00
⊖ 2014	
Qtr1	$1,148,861.00
Qtr2	$3,126,441.00
Qtr3	$2,021,263.00
Qtr4	$4,361,397.00
Grand Total	$32,064,332.00

Sorting By Largest Or Smallest

There are numerous times when the pivot table that you use has been set up fully, but you are unhappy with the way the data has been sorted. Another advantage of using a pivot table is that you can sort the data using any criteria. Let us first look at how we can sort the sum of sales for every year and quarter. Use the link provided at the start of the chapter to download the Excel workbook. The example below will explain to you how you can sort data based on the largest or smallest figure.

	A	B
6	Row Labels ▼	Sum of SALES
7	⊟ 2012	
8	Qtr1	$1,322,504.00
9	Qtr2	$1,676,623.00
10	Qtr3	$2,850,375.00
11	Qtr4	$4,538,744.00
12	⊟ 2013	
13	Qtr1	$1,523,771.00
14	Qtr2	$3,547,993.00
15	Qtr3	$2,380,031.00
16	Qtr4	$3,566,329.00
17	⊟ 2014	
18	Qtr1	$1,148,861.00
19	Qtr2	$3,126,441.00
20	Qtr3	$2,021,263.00
21	Qtr4	$4,361,397.00
22	Grand Total	$32,064,332.00

Step One: Right click on the Year cell in the pivot table, and choose sort newest to oldest.

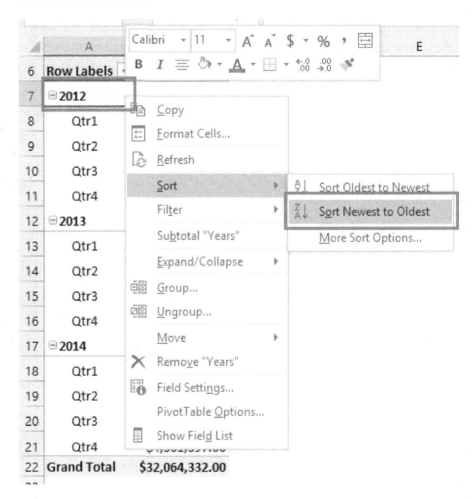

The data in the pivot is now sorted based on the years. If you look at the pivot, you will see that the data for 2014 appears first.

	A	B
6	Row Labels ↓	Sum of SALES
7	⊟2014	
8	Qtr1	$1,148,861.00
9	Qtr2	$3,126,441.00
10	Qtr3	$2,021,263.00
11	Qtr4	$4,361,397.00
12	⊟2013	
13	Qtr1	$1,523,771.00
14	Qtr2	$3,547,993.00
15	Qtr3	$2,380,031.00
16	Qtr4	$3,566,329.00
17	⊟2012	
18	Qtr1	$1,322,504.00
19	Qtr2	$1,676,623.00
20	Qtr3	$2,850,375.00
21	Qtr4	$4,538,744.00
22	Grand Total	$32,064,332.00

Step Two: Let us now see how we can sort the data on the basis of quarters. Go to the quarters in your pivot table and right click on them. Go to sort, and choose the 'Sort Newest to Oldest' option.

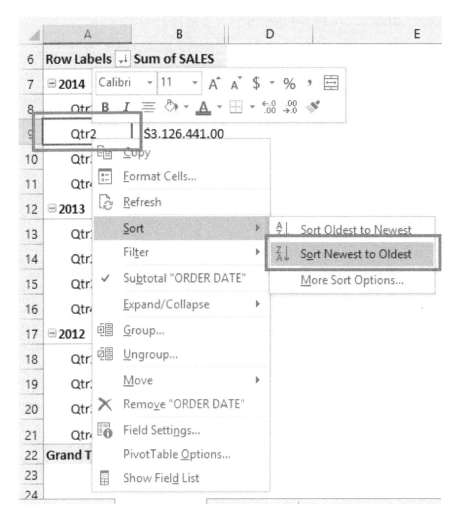

The quarters will now be sorted in descending order. If you look closely, you will see that the fourth quarter comes first in the list.

	A	B
6	Row Labels ↓	Sum of SALES
7	⊟ 2014	
8	Qtr4	$4,361,397.00
9	Qtr3	$2,021,263.00
10	Qtr2	$3,126,441.00
11	Qtr1	$1,148,861.00
12	⊟ 2013	
13	Qtr4	$3,566,329.00
14	Qtr3	$2,380,031.00
15	Qtr2	$3,547,993.00
16	Qtr1	$1,523,771.00
17	⊟ 2012	
18	Qtr4	$4,538,744.00
19	Qtr3	$2,850,375.00
20	Qtr2	$1,676,623.00
21	Qtr1	$1,322,504.00
22	Grand Total	$32,064,332.00

Step Three: Let us now look at what we can do with the column Sum of Sales. Right click on any value in the column, and select the Sort option. Now, sort largest to smallest.

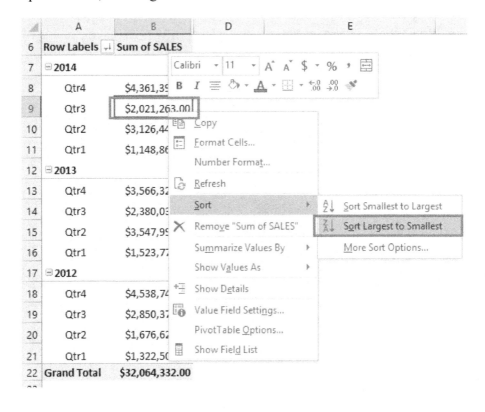

You can now see that the sum of sales has been sorted based on the descending order of the numbers.

	A	B
6	Row Labels ↓	Sum of SALES
7	⊟ 2014	
8	Qtr4	$4,361,397.00
9	Qtr2	$3,126,441.00
10	Qtr3	$2,021,263.00
11	Qtr1	$1,148,861.00
12	⊟ 2013	
13	Qtr4	$3,566,329.00
14	Qtr2	$3,547,993.00
15	Qtr3	$2,380,031.00
16	Qtr1	$1,523,771.00
17	⊟ 2012	
18	Qtr4	$4,538,744.00
19	Qtr3	$2,850,375.00
20	Qtr2	$1,676,623.00
21	Qtr1	$1,322,504.00
22	Grand Total	$32,064,332.00

It is amazing how a pivot table will allow you to sort the data in the source data based on your requirements.

Sort using custom Lists

It is always a good idea to use a custom list in Excel, especially if you want to add your personal list to the data. You can include different lists like phone numbers, regions, countries, customers or even work for every team member. The goal is to create a list to remove any repetitive work. It also helps to remove the probability of human error. Let us see how this can be done. Before we create a custom list, let us look at how we can use Excel's default list.

Step One: Type February in the first cell in the row.

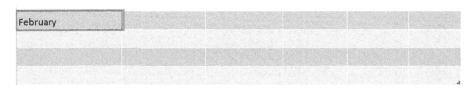

Step Two: Click the lower section of the cell and drag the cursor to the right by five cells.

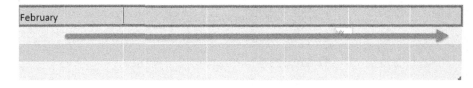

Step Three: Release the cursor and you will notice that the months have been populated automatically until July.

February	March	April	May	June	July

It may seem like magic when excel does this for you, but let us now look at how we can create custom lists in Excel.

Step Four: Go to the menu bar and select 'File.'

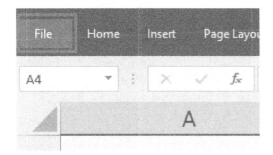

Step Five: Click on 'Options.'

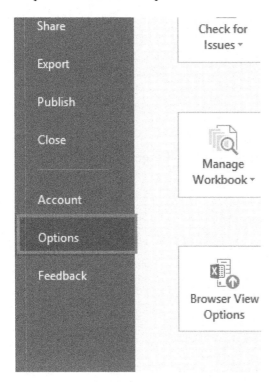

Step Six: Now choose the option 'Advanced.'

Step Seven: Click on edit Custom Lists in the general section of the dialog box.

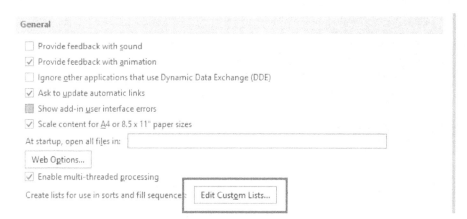

You will see the built-in lists of the days and months in the dialog box. When you click the custom list, you will see that the area under list entries is greyed out. This means that no changes can be made to that data. This means that this is a default custom list in Excel.

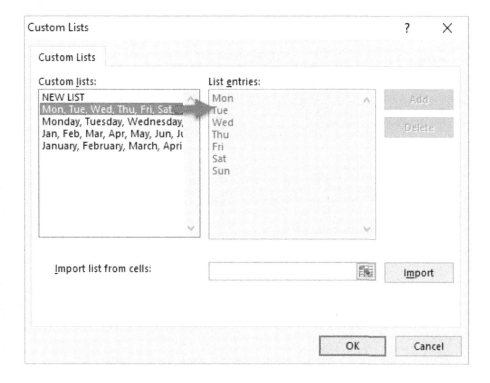

Step Eight: you can add or create a custom list in Excel under the List entries section. You should click on the new list option and enter the list manually. Remember that you can only enter one entry at a time.

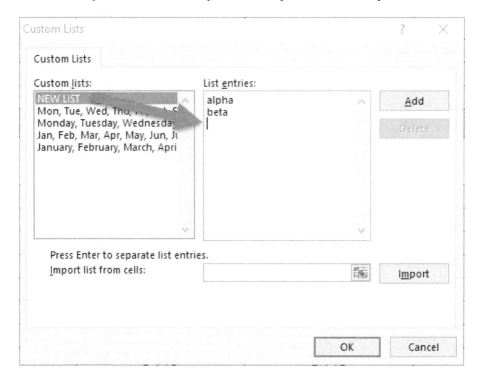

Once you have added the necessary values to the list, click Add. We have added the Greek alphabet to the list. Click OK when you are happy with the list.

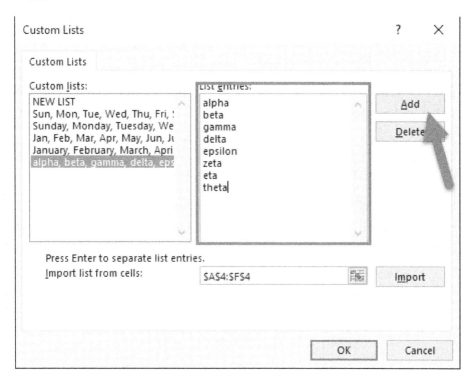

Step Nine: Click on OK.

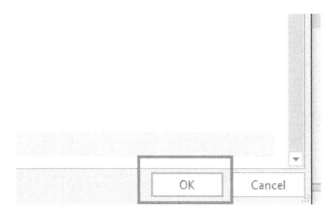

Step Ten: Let us now look at the previous Excel workbook to view the new custom list that is prepared. To see how this works, type alpha in one cell.

Step Eleven: Now click the lower right corner of your cell and drag the value to the cells on the right.

Step Twelve: Now release the cursor, and you will see that the data has been populated until zeta. This is based on the custom list that we created in the eighth step.

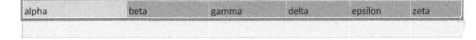

Filter by Dates

There are numerous date filters that you can choose from when you are using a pivot table. You can choose to filter by the week, the following month or quarter, the next year, last year or the current year. This list is endless. It is useful to use this option when you want to calculate the invoices for the data that you have collected. You can also use this to assess the sales. Let us first look at a few examples of filters.

Step One: Go to the Row Labels option, and select 'Date Filters.' Select the option 'Between' in the window that opens.

Step Two: Now, add the data range to the pivot table, and click OK.

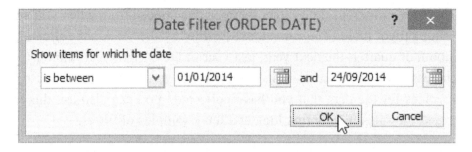

The data in the pivot table is filtered based on the dates.

Sum of SALES	Column Labels
Row Labels	2014
10/01/2014	53,586
09/02/2014	14,333
11/03/2014	29,570
10/04/2014	83,468
10/05/2014	25,263
09/06/2014	68,797
09/07/2014	49,562
08/08/2014	13,964
07/09/2014	23,798
Grand Total	362,341

Step Three: Let us now look at another example. Go to the Row Labels, and now filter based on the next quarter.

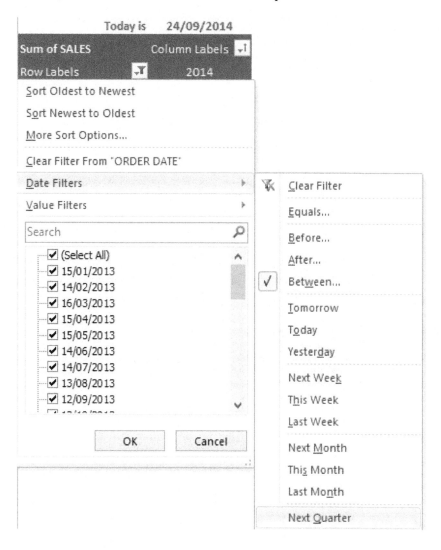

The pivot table is now filtered using the next quarter as the basis.

Sum of SALES	Today is	24/09/2014
	Column Labels	
Row Labels		2014
07/10/2014		16,843
06/11/2014		78,715
06/12/2014		80,780
Grand Total		176,338

Filtering by values

It is easy to filter a pivot based on the top ten values. You can choose from numerous value filters and perform different kinds of analysis. The image below shows the pivot table that we will be using.

Sum of SALES	Column Labels
Row Labels	2015
Acme, inc.	113,918
Demo Company	106,826
Widget Corp	94,378
Foo Bars	85,607
123 Warehousing	75,088
Fake Brothers	43,216
Smith and Co.	41,632
ABC Telecom	14,659
Grand Total	575,324

Step One: Move to the row labels and select value filters. Choose to filter based on the top ten values.

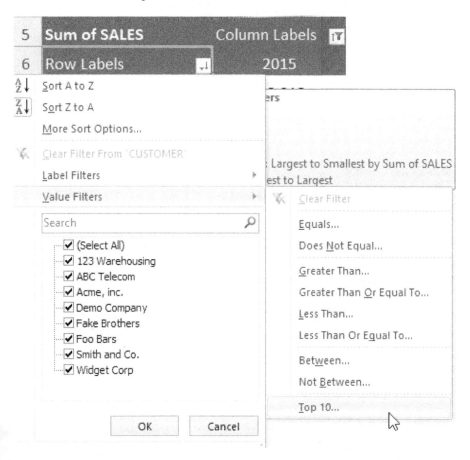

Step Two: Set the filter to the top five items and click ok.

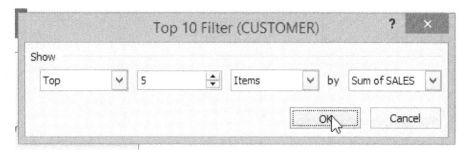

You have now added the required filters to the pivot table.

Sum of SALES	Column Labels
Row Labels	2015
Acme, inc.	113,918
Demo Company	106,826
Widget Corp	94,378
Foo Bars	85,607
123 Warehousing	75,088
Grand Total	475,817

Inserting Slicers

A slicer is an interactive and visual button or filter that allows you to look at the different items that have been chosen in a pivot table. Let us now look at how you can insert a slicer in your pivot.

Step One: Select any cell on your pivot table and click inside it.

Sum of SALES	Column Labels		
Row Labels	2013	2014	2015
123 Warehousing	66,826	49,562	75,088
ABC Telecom	67,320	108,285	14,659
Acme, inc.	85,030	25,263	113,918
Demo Company	113,799	13,964	106,826
Fake Brothers	66,663	164,248	43,216
Foo Bars	53,522	31,176	85,607
Smith and Co.	80,369	77,384	41,632
Widget Corp	129,462	68,797	94,378
Grand Total	662,991	538,679	575,324

Step Two: Go to Options or Analyze and choose to insert the slicer. You can select multiple fields. For the purpose of this exercise, we will look at the month and year fields. Click ok.

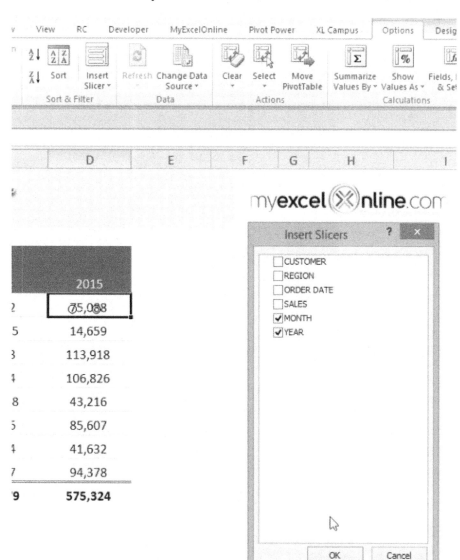

The slicer is now ready for you to use. You can slice and dice the data using the slicer. We will look at how you can select multiple slicers in your workbook in a different section.

Slicer Styles

There are numerous slicer styles that you can choose from. These styles will add some color to your Excel workbook. You can also add some components like columns to a slicer. If you want to explore the different styles that you can attach to a slicer, right click on a slicer and experiment with the different options that are available.

Step One: Select the slicer you want to update.

Step Two: In the menu bar, go to slicer tools and choose options. You can change the style of the slicer using the slicer styles option. You can always go back and make changes to the slicer is necessary.

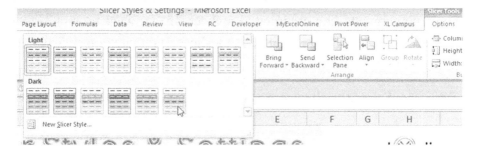

The pivot table slicer is now ready for you to use.

Slicer Connections between Multiple Pivots

The slicer that you insert to a pivot table will only be connected to that pivot table. So, what would you do if you had multiple pivot tables to work with? How would you connect the slicer to all the pivot tables so that one click can make a change across all pivot tables? You can do this by using the Report Connections or PivotTable connections option in Excel. This section will shed some light on how this can be achieved.

Step One: insert two pivot tables with the same structure as the images below.

Setup Pivot Table #1:

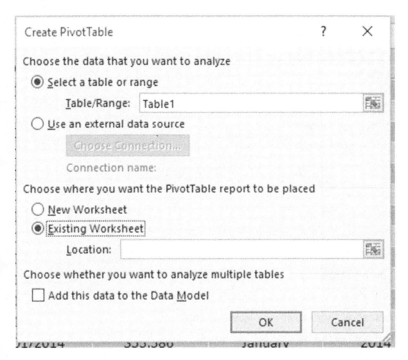

ROWS: Region

VALUES: Sum of Sales

Row Labels	Sum of SALES
EAST	381740
NORTH	423596
SOUTH	462942
WEST	508716
Grand Total	1776994

Setup Pivot Table #2:

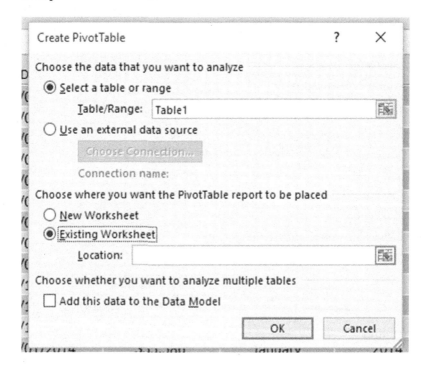

ROWS: Customer

VALUES: Sum of Sales

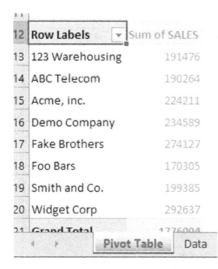

12	Row Labels	▾	Sum of SALES
13	123 Warehousing		191476
14	ABC Telecom		190264
15	Acme, inc.		224211
16	Demo Company		234589
17	Fake Brothers		274127
18	Foo Bars		170305
19	Smith and Co.		199385
20	Widget Corp		292637
21	Grand Total		1776004

◀ ▶   **Pivot Table**   Data

Step Two: Now, click on any cell in the first pivot table, and include the month slicer. You can do this by going to PivotTable Tools and selecting the option Analyze/Options. Next, click on 'Insert Slicer' and choose the base as Month. Click OK.

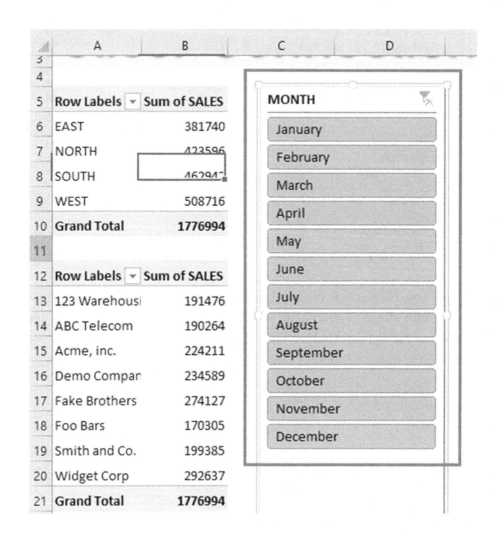

	A	B
5	Row Labels ▼	Sum of SALES
6	EAST	381740
7	NORTH	423596
8	SOUTH	462943
9	WEST	508716
10	Grand Total	1776994
11		
12	Row Labels ▼	Sum of SALES
13	123 Warehousi	191476
14	ABC Telecom	190264
15	Acme, inc.	224211
16	Demo Compan	234589
17	Fake Brothers	274127
18	Foo Bars	170305
19	Smith and Co.	199385
20	Widget Corp	292637
21	Grand Total	1776994

MONTH

January
February
March
April
May
June
July
August
September
October
November
December

Step Three: Now, click on any cell in the second pivot table, and include the year slicer. You can do this by going to PivotTable Tools and selecting the option Analyze/Options. Next, click on 'Insert Slicer' and choose the base as Year. Click OK.

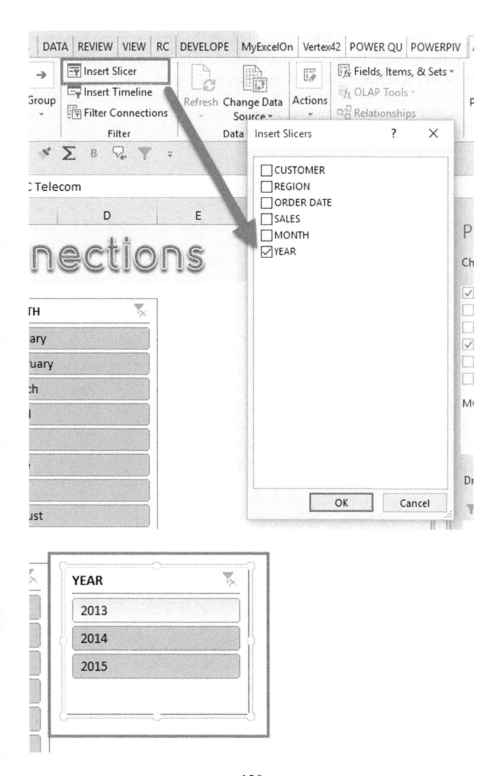

Step Four: You should now right click on the first slicer and then move to the report connections or pivot table connections. Select the box against PivotTable2 and then click ok.

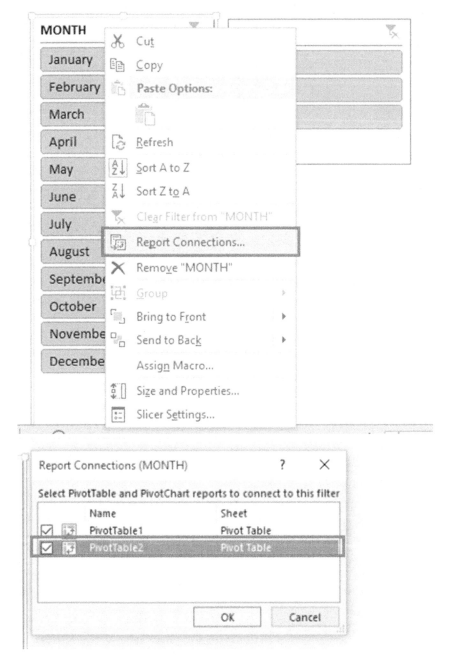

Step Five: Now, right click on the second slicer and move to the report connections or pivot table connections. Select the box against PivotTable1 and then click ok.

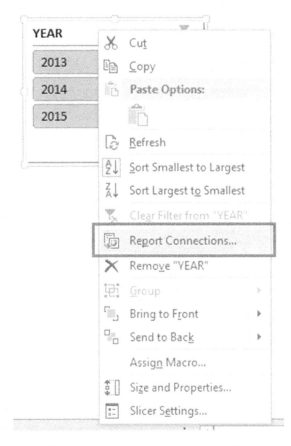

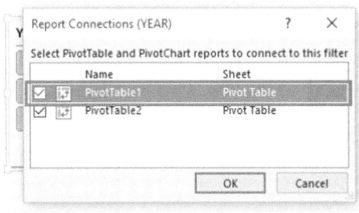

hen you select the items in the slicer, there will be a change in both pivot tables. Look at the image below, and the next section to see how you can perform this function.

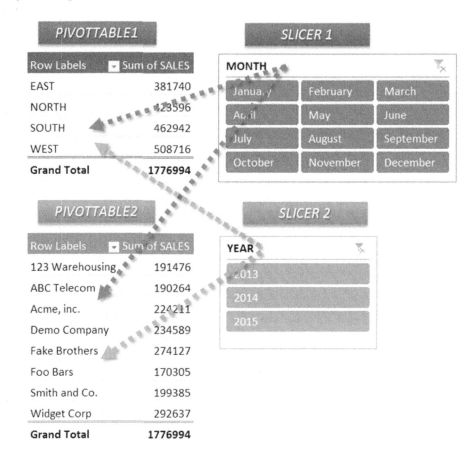

Filtering a Slicer

Excel allows you to slice your screen into different segments, and this is one of the best things about Excel. This feature was first introduced in the 2010 version, and they help you identify which items have been selected or filtered in a pivot. You can filter a slicer in different ways. Try practicing the different methods of filtering a slicer using the workbook provided at the beginning of the chapter.

Left Mouse Click

The easiest way to select numerous items in a slicer is by using the left mouse button.

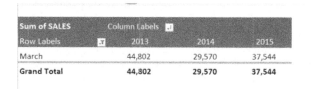

Drag Left Mouse Button

If you want to select numerous items in a slicer, you can drag the cursor down using the left mouse button.

Sum of SALES	Column Labels		
Row Labels	2013	2014	2015
January	26,884	53,586	56,959
February	46,174	14,333	47,189
March	44,802	29,570	37,544
April	49,049	83,468	53,413
May	80,369	25,263	20,816
Grand Total	247,278	206,220	215,921

Ctrl Keyboard

You can select numerous slicer items by holding the control key down and using the left mouse button to select the items.

Sum of SALES	Column Labels		
Row Labels	2013	2014	2015
January	26,884	53,586	56,959
Grand Total	26,884	53,586	56,9

134

Shift Keyboard

You should now select the first slicer item. If you want to select a second slicer item, hold the shift key down and press select. You can select a range of such items.

Sum of SALES	Column Labels		
Row Labels	2013	2014	2015
January	26,884	53,586	56,959
February	46,174	14,333	
March	44,802	29,570	
Grand Total	117,860	97,489	

MONTH

- January
- February
- March
- April
- May
- June
- July
- August
- September
- October
- November
- December

Creating Calculated Fields

In a pivot table, you can perform mathematical operations on the field list. You can perform different functions like addition, subtraction, multiplication and division. The only issue with this is that you are not allowed to reference any of the cells or values in the pivot. You can use this option to perform margin calculations, cost of goods sold or even the sales values. The pivot table on your screen should look as follows:

Row Labels	Column Labels 2014 Sum of SALES	Sum of COSTS
123 Warehousing	49,562	7,077
ABC Telecom	108,285	18,477
Acme, inc.	25,263	5,401
Demo Company	13,964	5,124
Fake Brothers	164,248	14,980
Foo Bars	31,176	17,431
Smith and Co.	77,384	15,967
Widget Corp	68,797	9,876
Grand Total	**538,679**	**94,333**

Step One: Click on a cell in the pivot table, and go to 'Options.' Now go to the section 'Fields, Items and Sets' and choose the 'Calculated Field' option.

Step Two: Now, set the name of the calculated field to Cost of Goods sold.

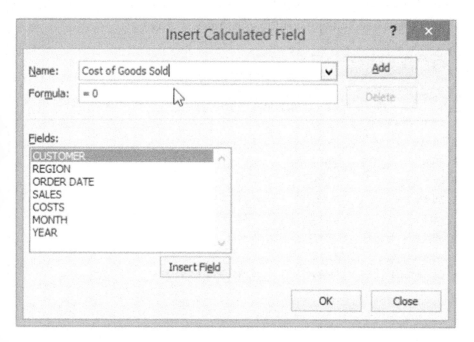

Step Three: Now add the formula in the dialog box. The values in the calculated field will be based on this formula.

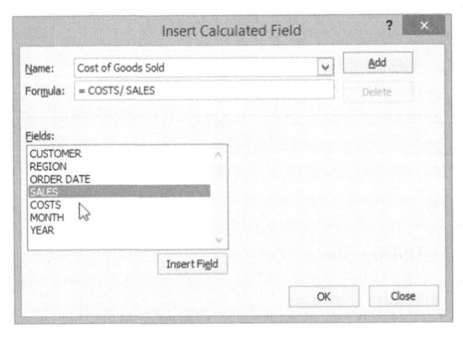

Step Four: Since the formatting is incorrect, you should right click on the column and select the option 'Number Format.'

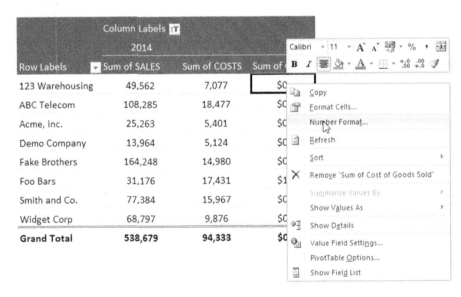

Step Five: Now, select the percentage option and click OK.

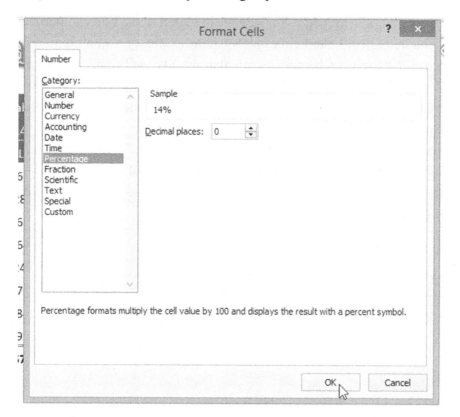

The new value is now in the percentage format and is ready to use.

Row Labels	Sum of SALES	Sum of COSTS	Sum of Cost of Goods Sold
123 Warehousing	49,562	7,077	14%
ABC Telecom	108,285	18,477	17%
Acme, inc.	25,263	5,401	21%
Demo Company	13,964	5,124	37%
Fake Brothers	164,248	14,980	9%
Foo Bars	31,176	17,431	56%
Smith and Co.	77,384	15,967	21%
Widget Corp	68,797	9,876	14%
Grand Total	538,679	94,333	18%

Creating Calculated Items in a Pivot

A Pivot table allows you to include a calculated item. You can perform any mathematical calculation on that item to obtain a new item. You can use different mathematical calculations like addition, subtraction, multiplication or division. The only issue with doing this is that you cannot refer to specific cells when you are performing these calculation operations. You can use this item to calculate changes between different records in the data set. If you want to create a calculated item, ensure that you click on the required cell in the pivot table. Now, move to the tab PivotTable Tools and go to Options. In this tab, select Fields, Items and Sets and choose Calculated Item.

Step One: Choose the item in the list that you wish to calculate.

Sum of SALES	Column Labels	
Row Labels	2014	2015
123 Warehousing	49,562	75,088
ABC Telecom	108,285	14,659
Acme, inc.	25,263	113,918
Demo Company	13,964	106,826
Fake Brothers	164,248	43,216
Foo Bars	31,176	85,607
Smith and Co.	77,384	41,632
Widget Corp	68,797	94,378
Grand Total	**538,679**	**575,324**

Step Two: Now, move to the tab PivotTable Tools and go to Options. In this tab, select Fields, Items and Sets and choose Calculated Item.

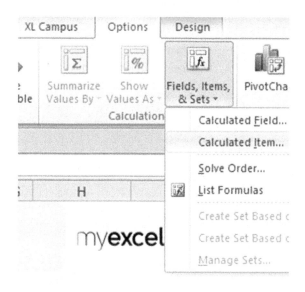

Step Three: Choose the Field Name 'Year on Year Variance.'

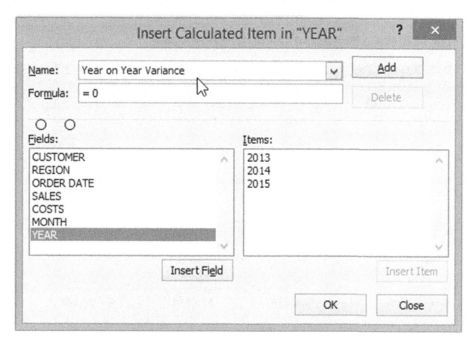

Step Four: Now, choose the formula that you want to use, and click ok.

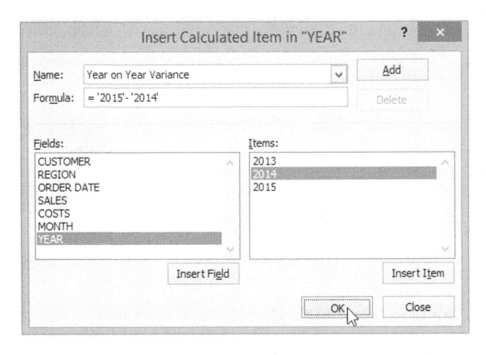

The item that you want to calculate is now ready.

Sum of SALES	Column Labels		
Row Labels	2014	2015	Year on Year Variance
123 Warehousing	49,562	75,088	25,526
ABC Telecom	108,285	14,659	-93,626
Acme, inc.	25,263	113,918	88,655
Demo Company	13,964	106,826	92,862
Fake Brothers	164,248	43,216	-121,032
Foo Bars	31,176	85,607	54,431
Smith and Co.	77,384	41,632	-35,752
Widget Corp	68,797	94,378	25,581
Grand Total	**538,679**	**575,324**	**36,645**

Insert a Pivot Chart

Pivot charts are an extension of pivot tables. They are used to represent the data present in a pivot table graphically. When you filter a pivot table, the chart will update automatically. If you want to insert a pivot chart in the worksheet, click on the pivot table and move to the tab labeled 'Pivot Table tools' and choose the 'Pivot Chart' option. You can achieve this easily in a few clicks, and will obtain a graphical representation of the pivot. The image below shows the pivot table that we are using.

Sum of SALES	Column Labels		
Row Labels	2013	2014	2015
EAST	134,146	157,847	89,747
NORTH	165,399	102,647	155,550
SOUTH	182,984	99,973	179,985
WEST	180,462	178,212	150,042
Grand Total	662,991	538,679	575,324

Step One: Click any cell in the pivot table and go to the options tab. Select PivotChart.

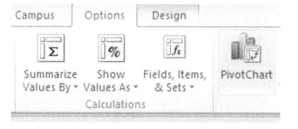

Step Two: A dialog box will appear and give you numerous chart types to choose from. Select a Chart type and click OK.

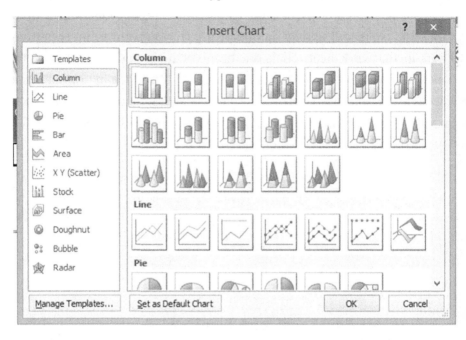

You will now see a pivot chart on your screen.

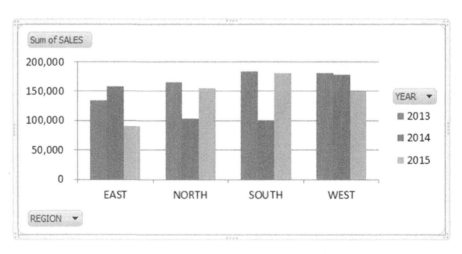

Pivot Chart and Slicers

Let us now take this a little further, and include a slicer in the pivot. You can use the slicer to control a pivot chart and the pivot table. Let us now look at how you can create an analytical report using a few steps. We have a pivot table and chart ready.

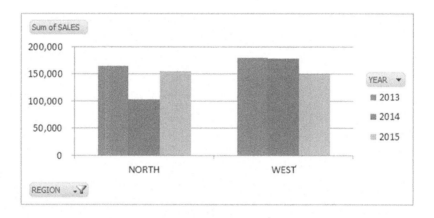

Sum of SALES	Column Labels		
Row Labels	2013	2014	2015
NORTH	165,399	102,647	155,550
WEST	180,462	178,212	150,042
Grand Total	345,861	280,859	305,592

Step One: Select a cell in your pivot table. Go to the Options tab and choose Insert Slicer.

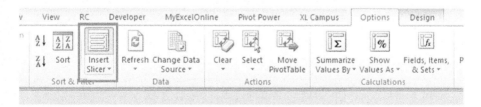

Step Two: Select the year and region.

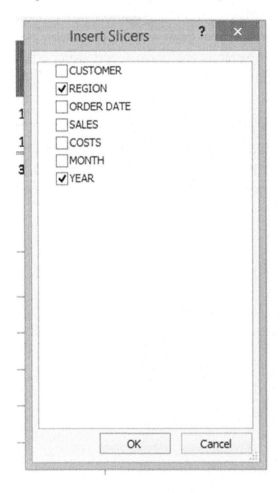

Excel will include the slicer in your pivot, and you can play around with the slicer. It is important to remember that this slicer will affect both your Pivot Chart and Pivot table.

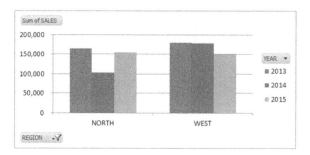

Highlight Cells Based on Their Values

One of the easiest ways to highlight cells in your data set based on the values present in those cells is to use a Conditional Formatting Rule. Conditional formatting allows you to visualize the results that you have obtained from your data set. You can make the conditional format interactive by assigning a criterion to a specific cell. When you manually change the value in the referenced cell, you will notice that the conditional format changes. Let us look at the image below:

Step One: Select a cell in the pivot table.

| Sum of SALES | Column Labels | | | HIGHLIGHT VALUES |
Row Labels	2013	2014	2015	BIGGER THAN...
January	26,884	53,586	56,959	50,000
February	46,174	14,333	47,189	
March	44,802	29,570	37,544	
April	49,049	83,468	53,413	
May	80,369	25,263	20,816	
June	53,522	68,797	85,607	
July	67,320	49,562	14,659	
August	66,663	13,964	43,216	
September	58,146	23,798	56,959	
October	83,288	16,843	47,189	
November	22,024	78,715	37,544	
December	64,750	80,780	74,229	
Grand Total	662,991	538,679	575,324	

Step Two: Go to the 'Home' tab and navigate to 'Conditional Formatting.' Click on the 'New Rule' option.

Step Three: Before you apply the rule, select the third option: 'All cells showing "Sum of SALES" values for "MONTH" and "YEAR"'.

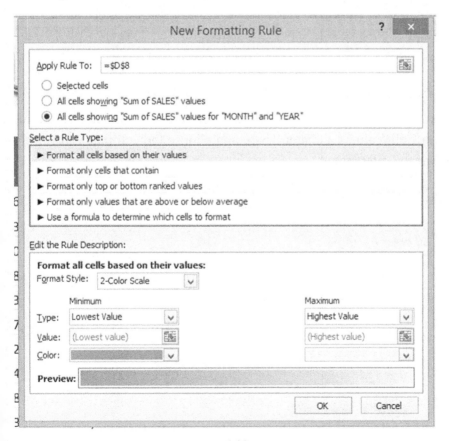

Step Four: Now, select the rule type 'Format Only Cells That Contain'.

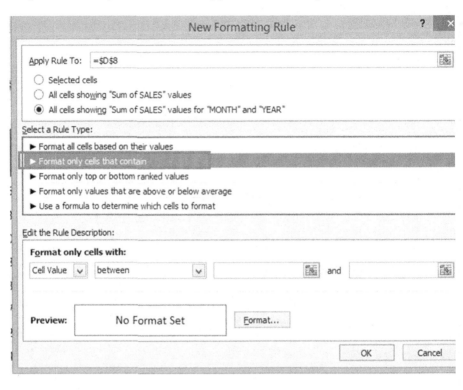

Step Five: Now, you should edit the description of the rule. To do this, go to Cell Value > Greater Than, and choose the cell that you want to use as the reference.

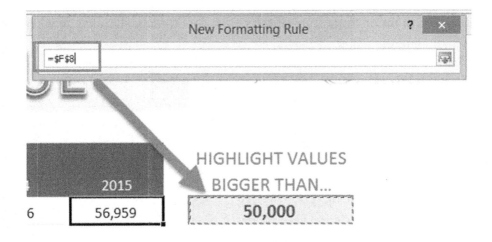

Step Six: Select the format and color.

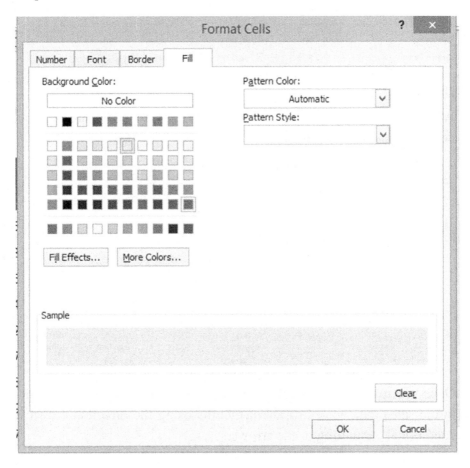

The highlight or formatting of the cell will automatically change when you update the value.

Sum of SALES	Column Labels				HIGHLIGHT VALUES
Row Labels	2013	2014	2015		BIGGER THAN...
January	26,884	53,586	56,959		80,000
February	46,174	14,333	47,189		
March	44,802	29,570	37,544		
April	49,049	83,468	53,413		
May	80,369	25,263	20,816		
June	53,522	68,797	85,607		
July	67,320	49,562	14,659		
August	66,663	13,964	43,216		
September	58,146	23,798	56,959		
October	83,288	16,843	47,189		
November	22,024	78,715	37,544		
December	64,750	80,780	74,229		
Grand Total	662,991	538,679	575,324		

Directional Icons

When you use a pivot table, it becomes easy to show the variance between the data collected.

	Column Labels					
	2012		2013		2014	
Row Label	Sum of SALES	Diff From Previous Month	Sum of SALES	Diff From Previous Month	Sum of SALES	Diff From Previous Month
January	771,186		872,080		1,074,820	
February	867,220	96,034	909,654	37,574	807,257	-267,563
March	784,136	-83,084	1,031,596	121,942	1,013,466	206,209
April	908,666	124,530	968,855	-62,741	836,559	-176,907
May	893,039	-15,627	850,502	-118,353	791,095	-45,464
June	786,918	-106,121	981,050	130,548	771,976	-19,119
July	1,056,573	269,655	854,835	-126,215	873,543	101,567
August	806,719	-249,854	1,002,597	147,762	599,246	-274,297
September	863,089	56,370	814,513	-188,084	1,011,288	412,042
October	873,208	10,119	931,193	116,680	1,059,308	48,020
November	923,402	50,194	769,352	-161,841	812,659	-246,649
December	854,090	-69,312	1,031,897	262,545	1,006,745	194,086
Grand Total	10,388,246		11,018,124		10,657,962	

Once you generate the pivot table, you can use it to show the variance in the sales data across different months using the directional icon in conditional formatting or the arrows.

152

Step One: Click on any of the values that calculate the variance in the pivot table and go to *Home > Conditional Formatting > Icon Sets > Directional*

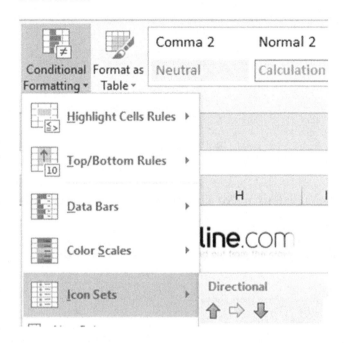

Step Two: You will now see the Apply Formatting Rule dialog box. Select the third option in the list and apply this formatting to every value except for the subtotal.

The pivot table will now look this way.

Column Labels						
	2012		**2013**		**2014**	
Row Labels	Sum of SALES	Diff From Previous Month	Sum of SALES	Diff From Previous Month	Sum of SALES	Diff From Previous Month
January	771,186		872,080		1,074,820	
February	867,220	96,034	909,654	37,574	807,257	-267,563
March	784,136	-83,084	1,031,596	121,942	1,013,466	206,209
April	908,666	124,530	968,855	-62,741	836,559	-176,907
May	893,039	-15,627	850,502	-118,353	791,095	-45,464
June	786,918	-106,121	981,050	130,548	771,976	-19,119
July	1,056,573	269,655	854,835	-126,215	873,543	101,567
August	806,719	-249,854	1,002,597	147,762	599,246	-274,297
September	863,089	56,370	814,513	-188,084	1,011,288	412,042
October	873,208	10,119	931,193	116,680	1,059,308	48,020
November	923,402	50,194	769,352	-161,841	812,659	-246,649
December	854,090	-69,312	1,031,897	262,545	1,006,745	194,086
Grand Total	10,388,246		11,018,124		10,657,962	

Step Three: Now we need to make some edits in the Conditional Formatting Rule in order to get the Icons right.

Go to *Home > Conditional Formatting > Manage Rules > Edit Rule*

154

Step Four: You will see the Edit Formatting Rule dialog box. Make the following changes in the dialog box:

Value = 0

Type = Number

"Check" the Show Icon Only box and press OK to confirm the changes:

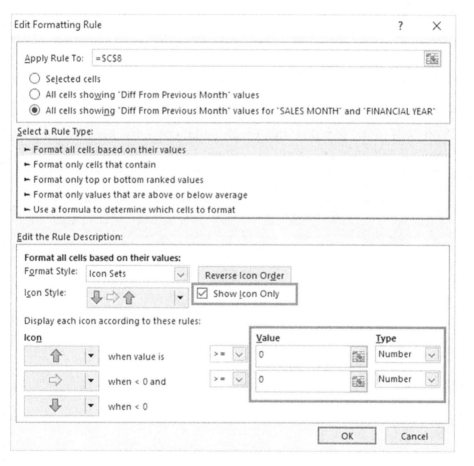

Step Five: You will now see another dialog box open, which is called the Conditional Formatting Rules Manager. Click the 'Apply' button and hit 'OK' to confirm the changes.

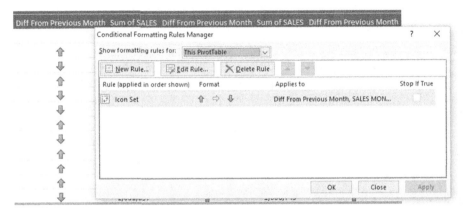

You will now see that the pivot table not only has the variance amounts but also shows the directional icons against the values in the cell.

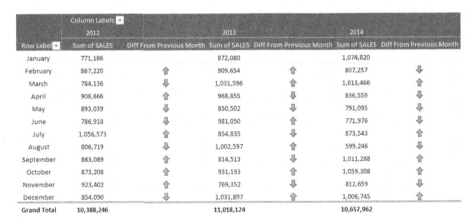

Data Bars, Color Scales & Icon Sets

The latest versions of excel have very good conditional formatting. The conditional formatting option includes color scales, icon sets and data bars.

Data Bars

Data bars include different forms of graphic bars that you can include in a cell. These bars are proportional to the value in the cell. This is a good tool to use for financial analysis.

Color Scales

Color scales allow you to add a background color to any cell. This color is proportional to the value in the cell. This is a good option to use if you want to generate heat maps.

Icon Sets

An icon set will allow you to show icons in a cell, and these icons also depend on the value of the cell. If you are preparing a project management report, you should use this option since it allows you to provide some detailed information.

Step One: You should first select the cells where you want to apply conditional formatting.

CUSTOMER	2013	2014	2015
Acme, inc.	£85,030	£25,263	£113,918
Demo Company	£113,799	£13,964	£106,826
Widget Corp	£129,462	£68,797	£94,378
Foo Bars	£53,522	£31,176	£85,607
123 Warehousing	£66,826	£49,562	£75,088
Fake Brothers	£66,663	£164,248	£43,216
Smith and Co.	£80,369	£77,384	£41,632
ABC Telecom	£67,320	£108,285	£14,659

Step Two: Navigate to the 'Home' Tab and go to Conditional Formatting Section of the tab.

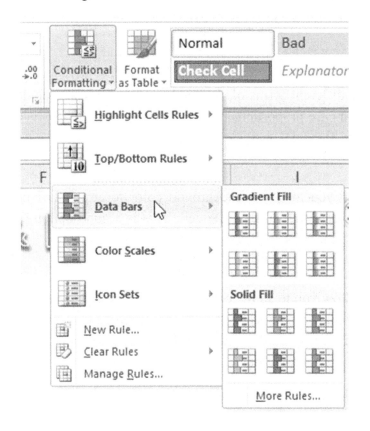

You can now choose a data bar, color scale or an icon set and see how this affects the selected range.

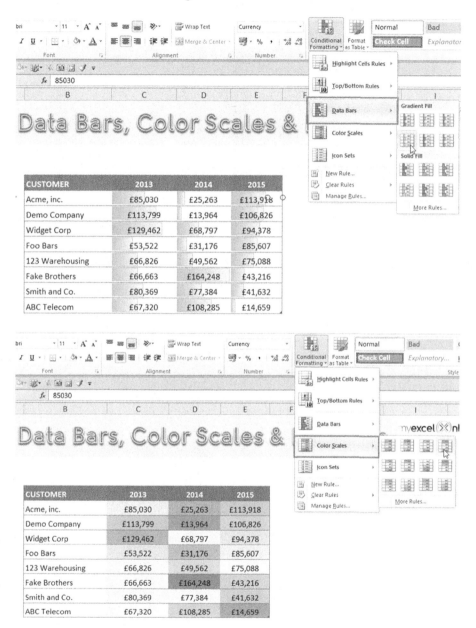

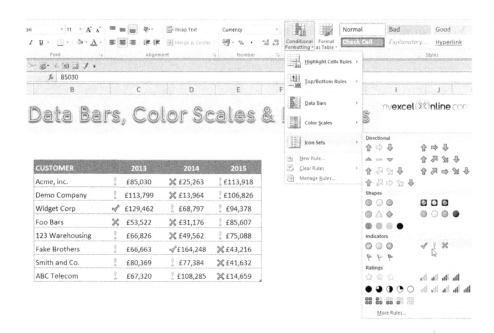

Data Bars, Color Scales & Icon Sets

CUSTOMER	2013	2014	2015
Acme, inc.	£85,030	£25,263	£113,918
Demo Company	£113,799	£13,964	£106,826
Widget Corp	£129,462	£68,797	£94,378
Foo Bars	£53,522	£31,176	£85,607
123 Warehousing	£66,826	£49,562	£75,088
Fake Brothers	£66,663	£164,248	£43,216
Smith and Co.	£80,369	£77,384	£41,632
ABC Telecom	£67,320	£108,285	£14,659

Chapter 4

Manipulating Data for a Pivot Table

Y ou may have created numerous Pivot tables when you were working on Microsoft Excel, but you may have encountered numerous problems while you were creating them. This is probably due to the fact that a pivot table is not as flexible as it should be or you may have had some trouble with connecting to the right data source. There are many different options that you can choose from when you are creating a Pivot table report. You must understand the different setting that you can use for this purpose. This chapter will take you through some of the issues that you may come across when you are using pivot tables.

Issues With Getting Started Your Company may have asked you to create a pivot table using the sales data for your company, but you are unsure of what issues or problems you will need to consider before you work on creating it. When you spend some time on planning, you will be able to create a pivot table that uses the right information and also delivers the right information that is required. You should consider the following when you plan on creating a pivot table:

- The type of data that you will be using to create the pivot table

- The location of the file

- The necessity to share the information with others

Accessing the Data

If your company asks you to create a pivot table to analyze the sales data of the company, you should first identify the type of information you will need to use. You can choose the source of the data for the analysis from the following options:

- Microsoft Excel list or database

- External data source

- Multiple consolidation ranges

- Another PivotTable report or PivotChart report

Most people choose to create a pivot table using one Excel list. Both the pivot and the data list can be found in the same workbook. Some pivots can be created using multiple lists or different sources like an analytical processing cube (OLAP), a database query or using a pivot table that is present in the same workbook. You should consider the following when you are creating a pivot table.

Where Is The Data Stored?

If you want to create a pivot table that will provide some meaningful insights, you should use accurate and current data. You should verify if the data being used to create the pivot table is indeed accurate and has been updated on a regular basis. You should identify whether the raw data is stored in another location. If there are other people who use the pivot table to obtain some meaningful insights, you should ensure that the pivot table is created in the same workbook as the data source. This will allow people to update the pivot with ease if there is a change to the data set.

How Frequently Will The Data Be Updated?

If you must update the raw data regularly you should ensure that you schedule a job that will automatically update or refresh the pivot table when the user opens the workbook. So, how will you notify Excel that it should refresh the pivot if the data is stored in an external data source?

What Issues Can You Or Other Users Face When You Have To Access Raw Data?

There are multiple issues that one can encounter when it comes to accessing raw data.

- Does every user have the accurate location of the source data?

- Does the pivot need to be refreshed at all times?

- Should all users have access to the password if the data is protected?

Source Data Fields

When you have sourced the data you will be using, you should ensure that it contains all the necessary fields. There are times when you may need to report on fields that are not present in the source data that you have obtained. For instance, if you need to analyze the sales data for your company and you need to plot the information regarding the variance between the budget and the plan, you must ensure that you have some information available in the source data to help you plot that information. You may need to calculate that information separately in the pivot table or add some additional fields to the source data. You must also assess the effect of performing either option on your analysis.

Shared Pivot Tables

The company may ask you to ensure that the data that you are creating is available to every employee in your company. There are, however, a few things that you will need to consider when you decide to share a pivot table with multiple people.

Does Every User Require The Same Detail?

There are some users, like the management, who will only need some top-level information. For instance, a senior executive may only want to see what the total sales are for a specific region. Other users may want some additional detail. A sales representative will need the data that is summed by product number or customer while a regional director will need data that is totaled by the district.

If the requirements vary, you will need to create numerous pivot tables where each pivot table is focused only on the needs of a specific set of users. If you cannot do this, you will need to create a pivot table that is simple. This will ensure that any user can navigate across the pivot table. You can also ascertain that the pivot table that you create can be tweaked or adapted to cater to the needs of different user groups.

Is The Data Sensitive?

Pivot tables often use sensitive information. For instance, the data set that you are using will contain both commission figures and sales results for every sales representative. If you want to create a pivot using that data set, you must know that any person who opens that workbook can view all the data that is present in the source. This will be the case even when you protect the worksheet or workbook. It is easy for people to crack passwords. This means that the protection can be bypassed easily by any other user. You should read the section 'About worksheet and workbook protection,' to understand more about this. This section can be obtained in Excel's help. This section of information will include a warning that states that a user can retrieve, obtain or modify the data in a workbook just by gaining some access to that data set. You should always use a strong password when you want to protect a workbook using a password.

When you create a pivot table using sensitive and confidential information, you must ensure that the pivot table only uses the data that a specific user is allowed to see. You can always create different lists in multiple workbooks and create a pivot using that list. This will mean that you will need to spend more time doing this, but it is an easy way to ensure data privacy. You can use different naming conventions or macros to standardize a pivot table or the source data. This will also minimize the work that you will need to put in to create an individual copy of the workbook. Alternatively, you can store these workbooks on secure network folders. This is because only authorized users have access to these folders.

Will you share the information in an electronic or printed format?

If you share information in the printed format you can reduce or completely remove the security issues. You can always control the information that is printed and given to a recipient. If you share the information electronically, you must ensure that you do not share some sensitive or confidential information with different users.

Will The Pivot Table Be Created In A Shared Workbook?

There are numerous features that you cannot use in a shared workbook. These include the creation or modification of a pivot table or chart. A user can only view a pivot table, but will not be able to rearrange these fields. The user will not be able to select different items in the dropdown list. Once you share a workbook with multiple users, you cannot change the protection. You also will not be able to run a macro, make changes to the macro or re-protect the worksheet.

Can Users Enable Macros In Your Workbook?

There are times when you will need to use a macro to improve the functionality of a pivot table. You must assess if you want users to have the ability to enable that macro in the workbook. There are some users who may be unable to use a macro in some environments. You must verify if this will have an impact on the analysis that users derive from the pivot table.

Preparing the Source Data

You must ensure that the source data that you are using is in the right format before you create a pivot table. The most common source of data for a pivot is a list in the workbook where the pivot table is created. You do not need to include too many records in the list, but you can also include thousands of records in the list. Regardless of what the size of the list is, there are some points that you must keep in mind when you are preparing the data set.

How Should The List Be Arranged To Create A Pivot Table?

1. There should always be a heading in the first row of the data set.

2. You should remove all blanks columns and rows in the list.

3. The data or records in each data set should have the same data type. For instance, if one column has currency, ensure that every record within that column has the same data type. The same holds true for other columns in the data set.

4. There are times when you may want to group data within the data set. You must ensure that the where you want to group the data has all the necessary fields.

5. You should always remove any calculations like totals, subtotals and group totals from the top or bottom of the list.

6. It is a good idea to name the range to make it easier for you to create a pivot table. There are times when the list will either increase or shrink. Therefore, it is recommended that you create a dynamic range.

7. If you notice that the subtotals feature has been switched on in the worksheet, you must remove it since Excel does not allow you to create a pivot table if the feature is on.

8. The auto filter feature does not affect the creation of a pivot table. This is because the pivot table will be created based on all the rows and columns within the data set regardless of whether they are visible or hidden.

9. If a row or a column has been hidden manually, it is okay to leave it hidden. This will not affect the creation of the pivot table for the same reason mentioned above.

Invalid Field Names

There are times when the wizard throws an error about there being invalid field names in the data set. This could be due to the fact that one or more headings in the data set are missing. You should ensure that you always select the required number of columns when you create a pivot table. As mentioned earlier, it is okay if some rows and columns are hidden. That being said, these hidden rows and columns can lead to some errors.

Using Filtered Data

You may have added some filters to the data set because you are looking only for specific information. The pivot table, however, contains all the records that are present in the data set. This is because the pivot table will include all the variables present in the data set even if there is an auto filter setting placed on the data set. Therefore, it is recommended that you use the auto filter option to obtain the required information and move that information into a different worksheet. You can then base the pivot table on the filtered list.

Using Data With Monthly Columns

There are times when you will have monthly data available in your data set, especially if you are using your company's sales data. It may be difficult to create a pivot table using this data since every month will have a field button of its own. It will be difficult to obtain annual totals in this instance. The data set does not include pivot field names, but includes pivot field item names. For instance, you may not have a data set that has the column heading month, but has a heading of its own. The data for that month is written in that column. It is a good idea to do this if you are looking to create a summary table. This method, however, is not useful when you create a pivot table. This is because you will have twelve data fields (one for each month), and will need to include another data field month that stores all the monthly data.

Therefore, you should rearrange the data into one column. This will help you create a flexible pivot since the data is normalized.

Let us assume that you are using a simple list. This list has the product names and the monthly sales figures. For this type of data set, follow the steps listed below:

1. Choose a cell in the list. Choose the option to select multiple consolidation ranges, select PivotTable as the report and click next.

2. Go to the 'Data' tab and select the 'PivotTable and PivotChart Report' option. Select the option 'I will create the page fields' and click next. Now, select the data set on your worksheet and choose the add button.

3. Let the remaining settings remain as the default settings. Click Next.

4. Now, choose the Layout button and in the dialog window that opens, drag every field except for the Sum of Value field from the pivot table. Click ok.

5. Now, click finish. You will see a pivot table appear in the workbook. You will see a Pivot table field list or pane on your screen that will contain the row, column and value field.

6. Double-click on the Grand total in the pivot, and add the underlying data to the pivot.

7. In the resulting Pivot, rename the headers to Product, Month and Amount.

Now, create a pivot using a normalized list where you will add product to the row area, month to the column area and amount to the value area.

Conclusion

Thank you for purchasing the book.

If you are someone who uses Excel at work to perform data analysis, you have come to the right place. This book will shed some light on what a pivot table is and also help you learn more about how you can perform data analysis using pivot tables. I hope the information in the book and the exercises in the book will help you work better with pivots.

Finally, if you enjoyed this book, then I'd like to ask you for a favor, would you be kind enough to leave a review for this book on Amazon? It'd be greatly appreciated!

Thank you and good luck!

Reference

https://blog.hubspot.com/marketing/how-to-create-pivot-table-tutorial-ht

https://webandsoftware.com/course/data-manipulation-reporting-with-pivot-tables-in-excel/

https://www.excel-easy.com/data-analysis/pivot-tables.html

https://www.freelancer.in/community/articles/50-possible-things-you-can-implement-on-excel-pivot-table

https://www.mrexcel.com/forum/excel-questions/268490-manipulating-data-pivot-tables.html

Made in the USA
Las Vegas, NV
21 December 2022

63792504R00098